BUREAUCRAZY

SULTAN A ALSHAALI

BUREAUCRAZY

The art of doing nothing

SULTAN A ALSHAALI

Bureaucrazy
Copyright © 2024 Sultan A Alshaali
First published in 2024

Print: 978-1-922456-80-9
E-book: 978-1-922456-81-6
Hardback: 978-1-922456-79-3

All rights reserved. No part of this book may be reproduced, stored in a retrieval system, or transmitted by any means (electronic, mechanical, photocopying, recording, or otherwise) without written permission from the author.

Because of the dynamic nature of the Internet, any web addresses or links contained in this book may have changed since publication and may no longer be valid. The information in this book is based on the author's experiences and opinions. The views expressed in this book are solely those of the author and do not necessarily reflect the views of the publisher; the publisher hereby disclaims any responsibility for them.

The author of this book does not dispense any form of medical, legal, financial, or technical advice either directly or indirectly. The intent of the author is solely to provide information of a general nature to help you in your quest for personal development and growth. In the event you use any of the information in this book, the author and the publisher assume no responsibility for your actions. If any form of expert assistance is required, the services of a competent professional should be sought.

Publishing information
Publishing and design facilitated by Passionpreneur Publishing
A division of Passionpreneur Organization Pty Ltd
ABN: 48640637529

Melbourne, VIC | Australia
www.PassionpreneurPublishing.com

TESTIMONIALS

Sultan is a natural-born leader who brings passion and energy to everything he works on. Sultan's multilingual, multicultural, and deep technical understanding of business gives him the ability to create instant bonds of trust with people he works with. Sultan also has the ability to create environments for people to succeed, even in the most complex and difficult situations, finding a win–win situation for every stakeholder.

Chuck Goldman
Co-Founder of Omnic Data, LLC.

Sultan is an extremely knowledgeable and professional industry leader I have had the honor to begin working with recently. With decades of experience in growth generation and investment sourcing, he is the ideal partner to help grow an enterprise or a market.

Parke Benjamin
COO/CFO at International Accelerator & CFO at IA Global Ventures Fund

I had the good fortune of working with Sultan in designing the operating model of an NGO. The one trait of Sultan which was so clear to everyone from the very beginning was that of leadership. With ease and panache, he assumed the leadership role in a diverse group of accomplished personalities. I felt a strong sense of authenticity in Sultan's style and a deep passion for the purpose of the NGO. He also took the lead in ensuring we all bonded as a team.

Neetan Chopra
Chief Digital and Information Officer at IndiGo

Sultan has a positive energy that flows so beautifully in his work. He has a manner that is both charismatic and professional in his way of conducting business. I had the opportunity to work with Sultan during his time in the Prime Minister's office and I found him to be very cooperative and supportive in team work-related activities. He has a leadership style that is calm and caring towards others.

Sarah Shaw
Senior Advisor at COP28 UAE

This book is dedicated to those whose hard work often goes unnoticed but plays a vital role in progress.

ACKNOWLEDGEMENTS

I am deeply grateful for the invaluable contributions of mentors, colleagues, leaders, and friends throughout my diverse professional journey. Their guidance, support, and collaborative spirit have shaped my career and personal growth. This book stands as a tribute to the collective efforts and meaningful connections that have enriched my experiences.

Thank you to everyone who has played a role in this remarkable adventure.

TABLE OF CONTENTS

Testimonials v
Acknowledgements ix
Introduction xiii

Chapter 1
THE ENIGMA OF UNEARNED SUCCESS 1

Chapter 2
NAVIGATING THE CORPORATE CHESSBOARD 14

Chapter 3
HOW TO DO NOTHING 19

Chapter 4
HOW TO DO NOTHING AND GET PROMOTED 41

Chapter 5
HOW TO BE SAFE 60

Chapter 6
HOW TO BLAME OTHERS AND BE SAFE 77

Chapter 7
HOW TO CLAIM CREDIT FOR
YOUR COLLEAGUES' WORK 92

Chapter 8
HOW TO CLAIM CREDIT FOR EVERYONE'S WORK 110

Chapter 9
HOW TO BE A SYCOPHANT 126

Chapter 10
HOW TO BE A SUPER-SYCOPHANT... 143

Chapter 11
HOW TO BETRAY NUMBER TWO AND WIN 153

Chapter 12
HOW TO BETRAY NUMBER ONE AND WIN.......................... 166

Chapter 13
HOW TO FIND A BETTER JOB BEFORE
THEY DISCOVER YOU'VE BEEN DOING
NOTHING ALL THESE YEARS 177

Chapter 14
HOW 'BUREAUCRAZY' ARE YOU?... 197

Conclusion 207
Author Bio...208

INTRODUCTION

Welcome to the world of *Bureaucrazy—The Art of Doing Nothing*, where the pursuit of professional excellence takes an unconventional twist. If you've ever felt the desire to master the subtle and often-overlooked art of navigating the corporate maze with finesse, this book is your roadmap to success.

In the age of efficiency, the chapters are not about hard work; they're about *smart* work—or perhaps, hardly any work at all. As you delve into the pages of this book, you'll find yourself nodding along, recognizing the absurdities of office life, and realizing that, yes, this book is for you.

Through engaging chapters like 'How to Do Nothing and Get Promoted' and 'How to Blame Others and Be Safe', this book offers a strategic roadmap for navigating corporate chaos with elegance. From claiming credits for others' work to mastering the art of sycophancy and betrayal, each chapter unveils the subtleties of bureaucratic success.

So, whether you're a seasoned bureaucrat looking to refine your skills or a newcomer eager to navigate the maze of office politics, *Bureaucrazy* beckons you to embrace the absurdities and excel in the fine art of doing nothing. It's not just a book—it's your secret weapon for success in the world of bureaucratic madness.

CHAPTER 1
THE ENIGMA OF UNEARNED SUCCESS

Once upon a time in a busy city, there lived a hardworking and dedicated employee named Alex. He worked tirelessly at a corporation, pouring his heart and soul into his job. Despite his hard work, Alex often went unnoticed by his superiors, overshadowed by more vocal colleagues.

One day, Alex discovered that his credit had been stolen many times by a cunning co-worker named Mark. Shocked and devastated, Alex felt betrayed and helpless. But instead of succumbing to despair, he decided to take matters into his own hands.

With determination in his heart, Alex embarked on a journey to reclaim his stolen identity. He tirelessly gathered evidence, sought advice, and reached out to his superiors. He encountered many obstacles and setbacks along the way, but his unwavering spirit kept him going.

As news of Alex's struggle spread, his colleagues started to take notice. Inspired by his resilience and determination, they rallied behind him, offering their support and assistance.

Alex's case gained widespread attention, and the truth was unveiled. Mark's deceitful actions were exposed for all to see. The corporation took swift action, transferring Mark to another department with a promotion and a raise ... as well as swiftly terminating Alex's services.

Alex's story inspired all his colleagues to stay quiet and never speak again in fear of being terminated as well.

The end ...

Even though this story is fictional, I and many other people can say that they've lived it, witnessed it, or heard of something similar happening to someone else—simply because 'Marks' do exist, and come in different shapes and forms.

You know exactly who they are. They're the ones to whom people point and ask, 'How did *they* get that job?' The answer's often a shrug at best, an expletive-laden rant at worst. They're the mouth-breathers, the ones who contribute next to nothing at work but somehow manage to suck up all the oxygen in the room and take all the credit for everyone's work except their own.

These people make themselves look good when it matters most, thereby elevating themselves far above everyone else in the eyes of their superiors. As a result, they have apparent success and manage to get themselves promoted—all while stepping over the bodies of the people who legitimately deserved those promotions.

How exactly do people like that do what they do? What makes them so successful? What makes them tick? This book will answer all those questions and more.

I've always encouraged open communication to foster a culture of transparency, fairness, and ethical behavior throughout my professional career. My simple request to both colleagues and subordinates was to keep me updated if the subject at hand is related to our scope of work, as well as to let me know if I can contribute one way or another. I would sometimes jump through the email chain with feedback or comments, especially if I had something to add or spotted a mistake requiring intervention.

One day, I get a meeting request from my 'boss' to discuss a proposal that was submitted from my department. The proposal title sounded familiar, as we'd discussed it in our department meeting but never actioned it or assigned it to any team member to work on. This left me a bit confused, but I had no time to investigate since I was in a workshop and the meeting was scheduled immediately after.

As I made my way to the meeting room, I asked another member of my team if they were aware of this. They replied that it just popped up on the calendar while we were in the workshop. Looking at the email meeting invitation attendees list, I immediately recognized who from my department was behind this—the newest team member, who'd been recently transferred from another department. Even though we had multiple discussions as a team about different concepts and proposals to pitch to the boss for approval, I wasn't ready for what came next.

I sat next to 'the boss' in the meeting room. When asked what this was about, I admitted that this meeting was scheduled without my knowledge and was also eager to know more. So, we were already in an awkward situation from the beginning.

The employee thanked us for our time in advance and started immediately with the most bizarre presentation I've ever attended. It was a mashup of all the ideas discussed within the department that haven't been completely developed from a concept into a proposal. Moreover, everything was presented without citing or crediting any of the team members that initially proposed the ideas.

There were also a few slides at the end of the presentation with a strange proposal. The content made sense when read separately, yet didn't add up to a solid conclusion. Thankfully, this triggered the boss to call an end to the meeting and ask the employee to come back with a more mature concept for the last proposal without commenting on all the previous slides.

Little did that employee know, I had a weekly check-in meeting with the boss which didn't take more than half an hour. During these meetings, I gave an update on progress and discussed new concepts. I did, however, credit each idea to the team member proposing it, ensuring the boss was completely aware of each idea and its originator.

Further, I requested a copy of the presentation after the meeting. Later that day, I noticed some inconsistencies in the language used to convey the concepts of the last proposal in the presentation. My gut feeling was confirmed when I ran the text through a plagiarism website and found that 98% of the content was copied from multiple websites. (The paragraphs had been moved around, which is why the proposal ended up being incoherent and confusing.)

What was it that drove such an employee that I considered an expert within the organization, and supposedly a veteran with decades working with different entities, to plagiarism?

If a highly competitive organization lacks a strong ethical culture, employees may feel pressured to outshine their peers. This pressure can lead some to gain an edge by resorting to unethical means. Some individuals have an intense desire for recognition and rewards. They may feel that taking credit for others' work will lead to greater acknowledgment and praise from superiors or colleagues. In some cases, employees might be afraid of failure or negative consequences, pushing them to take credit for work they didn't do to maintain a high profile and avoid potential repercussions.

Unethical employees may believe that taking credit for others' achievements will enhance their chances of receiving promotions, salary increases, or other career advancements. They might feel that by appearing more successful, they can secure their position within the company and protect themselves from downsizing or layoffs.

Individuals with low self-esteem may resort to taking credit for others' work to compensate for their perceived inadequacies. Seeking validation from others can drive some individuals to engage in deceptive practices to boost their self-worth.

The objective of this book is to expose the tricks these immoral employees utilize to advance their careers without adding value to the organization.

It took me many years and countless experiences, including personal encounters and direct observations, to recognize that addressing this issue isn't as complex as it may seem. Fundamentally, the success of individuals who thrive on taking credit for others' work can be effectively shortened by implementing proper preventive measures.

In general, the strategies of such employees revolve around destroying the moral compass of the organization as well as taking advantage of colleagues—their fellow employees, including those at the same level as they are, those who work under them, and even (to a certain extent) those who rank more highly than they do.

Who'll benefit from reading this book?

By reading this book, you'll learn all the strategies employed by these kinds of people. You'll thus be empowered to better protect yourself from being taken advantage of by their immoral yet maddeningly effective tactics. Not only will you be able to prevent yourself from being stepped on and used by these people, but you'll also be able to take a leaf out of their book by studying the positive aspects of their tactics. Not every facet of what they do is wrong. Some of what they do is actually healthy, useful, and practical; they just take certain healthy practices and overuse or twist them to their advantage.

By no means should you feel compelled to imitate everything these immoral workers do. But by studying their mindset and their strategies, you'll not only be better-equipped to safeguard yourself against being hurt by them in the workplace, but you'll also learn the positive aspects of their tactics and know-how to live a healthier, more successful, more fulfilling life.

If you're an employee required to work with others in the same organization daily or regularly, this book's for you. You might think, *Wait, why do I need this book? I really don't have any coworkers who would do this kind of thing to me.* If this is genuinely the case, I'm exceedingly happy for you.

But there's no guarantee that Human Resources or one of your company's other departments won't become enchanted with such a person in the future and hire them to work on your team, under you, or even as your superior. So, you need to prepare yourself for this eventuality. And the best way to do this is to study this type of person and the tactics, mindset, and strategies they employ.

So, unless you're independently wealthy (and thus have no need to work), self-employed, or working in a very small company in which you're perhaps the only employee (and it's unlikely that other employees will be hired in future), this book's for you. Basically, everyone with coworkers (now or in future) can benefit from this book. Even if you're the boss or the head of an organization, you'll still benefit by learning how to detect these immoral employees and avoid hiring them (since they'll ultimately fail to add any value to your organization).

WHAT WILL YOU GET FROM READING THIS BOOK?

By using this book to study this type of immoral employee and the tactics, mindset and strategies they employ, you'll be able to recognize the warning signs early on and take appropriate steps to protect yourself. You'll know how to take proactive measures to prevent this person from being undeservedly promoted in the organization, and from taking advantage of others' work to achieve the successes which rightfully belong to you or someone else more deserving.

Further, you'll learn how to keep yourself and your coworker from getting stabbed in the back by these sorts of people. If you find it necessary, you may even feel obligated to expose these people for what they are (using the knowledge contained in this book) to those in charge, so that these toxic employees are purged from the organization to make room for those adding actual value.

One other aspect of the help you may derive from this book lies more on the positive side. You'll learn the benefits of applying some of the strategies used by those immoral employees, but in moderation.

WHAT ACTIONS SHOULD YOU TAKE AFTER READING THIS BOOK?

There are several lanes open to you after digesting the information found in this book, which you'll learn in later chapters.

You could do nothing.

The first option for what you might do after reading this book is to do nothing. If you don't currently have coworkers who'd try to take advantage of you or others in the manner described in the book, and you're not thinking of hiring anyone who might fit this description, one option is simply to file away what you've learned in the depths of your brain and retrieve this information only when it's applicable to your life (such as when you're actually faced with such an employee or prospective hire).

You could apply some of the more positive aspects for your own benefit.

Another option is to take some of the more positive aspects of the strategies that these immoral employees utilize and apply them to your own life and career. Selectively applying certain aspects of their strategies in the right doses can allow you to achieve a better, healthier work–life balance and help you work smarter.

You could play defense.

Another viable path to take after reading this book is using it to defend yourself against any employees who'd use such tactics against you. If you know the playbook of the enemy and every strategy contained within it, you'll know *exactly* what they're trying to do. This will enable you to prevent them from taking advantage of you, stealing the credit for your work, and stepping all over you on their way to the top. You can become an immovable barrier in their path to what they thought would be easy success.

Further, not only can you use the information in this book to defend yourself against the strategies used by these immoral employees, but you can also teach others in your workplace—those who deserve to benefit from this knowledge—to defend themselves in the same way. This will ensure that those adding value to your organization don't get taken advantage of or treated unfairly, and also that people who don't add value fail to move up any higher than they should.

If you work in a supervisory or managerial capacity and/or control the hiring and firing decisions, you can use the information contained in this book to make smarter personnel decisions. It will help you identify those who aren't adding currently value to your organization, or who are unlikely to do so in future. After all, the people you want working for you are those who'll pull their own weight.

You could play offence.

Another path you could take (one which you may find necessary) is to use the contents of this book to play offence. Since you'll soon know the exact strategies these immoral employees take in building themselves up and bringing everyone else down, you can use this knowledge to turn the tables, exposing them to your fellow employees, managers, and supervisors.

If you reveal to your coworkers and those in charge that the troublesome employees in your workplace are in fact lazy, do-nothing, mouth-breathing, oxygen sucking, backstabbing workers, they may actually lose their positions, saving your organization money and making room for individuals who'll add value to your company and help everyone to succeed, grow, and thrive.

Ultimately, the decision lies with you.

Of course, whatever path you decide to follow after reading this book is ultimately your choice. Having now learned the strategies of immoral employees, you could even seek to become one of them by emulating their tactics and their mode of thinking. This book will indeed thoroughly equip you with all the tools to do so. It's your choice. It is, after all, an easy (though perhaps unfulfilling and somewhat degrading) career path.

However, I tend to think that those who are the bearers of such valuable information ought to put it to good use. It's possible that you may be lucky enough never to encounter an immoral employee such as the one described in this book. But honestly, the odds are low. And even if you never encounter such an employee throughout the course of your career (and thus never have to use the information contained in this book to defend yourself against their immoral tactics), you might have a friend or a family member who has to work with such an employee and is suffering as a result of this civil unrest. In such a case, you can use your knowledge to help them escape their situation or equip them with the knowledge to defend themselves.

Even if you're never faced with the unsavory prospect of safeguarding yourself from being stabbed in the back by one of these employees, you can still use the information in the following chapters to apply some of these principles. Used in moderation, they can help you work smarter and more profitably, achieve a better work-life balance, and become healthier, less stressed, and more efficient in everything you do. When used wisely, these principles can empower you to add maximum value to your organization with minimum effort, leading to a more fulfilling and relaxed life.

And that, my friend, is the gold standard.

CHAPTER 2

NAVIGATING THE CORPORATE CHESSBOARD

Step into the Big Picture chapter, where the panoramic view unfolds to reveal the intricate web of workplace shenanigans. From the art of doing nothing to the fine nuances of betrayal, this chapter offers a bird's-eye perspective of the tactics employed by immoral employees.

Explore the twisted minds behind such tactics, as we explore the dark arts of career advancement, blame-shifting, credit-stealing, sycophancy, and strategic betrayals. Get ready for a revealing journey through the corporate maze, where every page unveils a new layer of 'bureaucrazy'.

It's time to decode the secrets of professional survival and manipulation. Are you prepared for the shocking revelations that lie ahead?

In today's dynamic and competitive corporate landscape, navigating the intricacies of professional survival and understanding the subtle art of corporate manipulation have become vital for individuals striving to thrive in their careers. Beyond mastering job-specific skills, the ability to decipher the unwritten rules of the corporate world is a crucial aspect of safeguarding oneself professionally and psychologically.

The modern workplace is not only a battleground for talent but also a terrain where interpersonal dynamics, office politics, and strategic maneuvering play pivotal roles. Learning the secrets of professional survival equips individuals with the tools to anticipate challenges, seize opportunities, and build resilience in the face of adversity.

Moreover, understanding the nuances of corporate manipulation is essential for protecting one's mental and emotional wellbeing, fostering a healthy work–life balance, and ensuring long-term career sustainability. As the saying goes, knowledge is power—and in the corporate arena, this knowledge is the key to safeguarding one's professional and psychological integrity.

Delving deeper in the next two chapters, I'll examine the concept of doing nothing and the benefits it can provide for your health as well as the fact that doing nothing may (somewhat counterintuitively) end up making you more efficient than you'd otherwise be. The second chapter more closely examines how to 'do nothing and get promoted' by revealing how doing nothing allows you to become more aware of any opportunities for advancement that may arise.

Chapters 5 and 6 explore the mindset behind playing it safe. Specifically, Chapter 5 reveals how avoiding conflict and staying neutral in your place of work, exercising empathy, and looking busy will allow you to stay safe. Chapter 6 then goes over how one can play it safe in their place of work by placing the blame on other people, especially by lying and attacking other colleagues.

Chapters 7 and 8 discuss how these immoral employees end up claiming credit for work that they didn't do, whether it's the work of their colleagues or that of anyone else. They successfully steal credit and ideas from those around them (often without their colleagues even noticing), then work that to their advantage. Generally, this theft of intellectual property happens without anyone raising a single objection.

Chapters 9 and 10 examine how to be a sycophant, defined as a self-seeking, servile, insincere flatterer or someone who acts in an obsequious manner toward another person offering an important path to gaining favor and advantage. Chapter 9 studies the concept of sycophancy in a broader sense, while Chapter 10 offers a deep dive into those who are sycophants in the extreme, those who'll do anything to please people in power for personal gain.

Chapters 11 and 12 contain a disturbing, yet revealing, portrait of how these immoral employees can betray those above them and come out on the winning side. Specifically, Chapter 9 teaches you how they betray Number Two (the second in command) and still come out on top, and Chapter 12 demonstrates how they manage to betray Number One (the person with the highest position and theoretically the most power) and *still* end up winning.

Chapter 13 provides invaluable insights into how these immoral employees are ultimately able to get away with what they do undetected and thrive—they secure a better job at a different organization before anyone discovers the fact that they've been doing nothing at all for several months or even years on end. The chapter explores how they often succeed at doing so simply because they're willing to try to apply for new jobs and find other targets who'll be even more vulnerable to their tactics.

Chapter 14 asks a fundamental question: How 'bureaucrazy' are you? It examines the principle of bureaucracy in the context of the working environment and demonstrates how it provides a safe zone for those who rely on it by engendering a predictable, stable, and repetitive work structure.

A FEW LAST THOUGHTS ON WHAT YOU'LL DERIVE FROM READING THIS BOOK.

After exploring these myriad yet related topics of discussion in depth, you'll be fully informed on exactly how these immoral employees function, how their brains work, what their thoughts are, what their strategies will be, and what their next moves will be.

This knowledge will provide you with the means to protect yourself and your co-workers from being taken advantage of by these types of people. Hopefully, this knowledge will keep these people from pulling the wool over your eyes, as well as over the eyes of your boss. It will even enable you to go on the offensive and eliminate these types of employees from your organization in order to make your place of business more productive and successful.

CHAPTER 3

HOW TO DO NOTHING

> *People say, 'Nothing is impossible,'
> but I do nothing every day!*
>
> — WINNIE-THE-POOH

In this chapter, let's start by discovering the surprising perks of 'doing nothing' while navigating the thin line between idleness and self-esteem.

We'll discuss how 'doing nothing' can actually be good for you, while imposing certain limitations on yourself—because doing absolutely nothing *all the time* can cause severe damage to your self-esteem.

Further, it's not always easy to find exactly the right level of balance between 'doing nothing' and 'doing something'. Also, doing nothing can have different meanings for different people. So, let's dive in and explore this controversial subject.

WHAT EXACTLY DOES 'DOING NOTHING' MEAN?

In the context of this book, to do nothing (at its most basic level) is to be idle and unproductive. Doing nothing means that you're not working toward a tangible goal or the production of a service or a product that would be considered a useful contribution to the economy or the world at large. Winnie-the-Pooh, by contrast, isn't technically doing absolutely nothing all day. He's breathing, singing, rummaging, eating his own honey, moseying about, visiting friends, conversing with those friends, stealing and eating the honey of those friends, and searching for more honey. But what Winnie-the-Pooh does is *considered* to be nothing due to the fact that his activities don't make a useful contribution to society; that is, his activities don't *add value*.

Doing nothing can also include procrastinating. As many of us may know, when we're procrastinating, we're often extremely productive at accomplishing a lot of things—everything except that which we're supposed to be doing. For instance, if you're working from home and you have a project which needs to be finished within two days, you may find that during that time, doing just about anything else—cleaning the house, running errands, fixing the grill, vacuuming, cleaning the swimming pool, helping your kids with their math homework, getting the leaves and mud out of the gutter, etc.—is more appealing to you than the work project you're required to complete and which is due very soon. You may find yourself utterly willing and easily able to complete many other necessary and mundane tasks (as long as they're not the work project with its looming deadline).

So, doing nothing means being idle and failing to make any progress toward accomplishing the task to which you've been assigned or which you've set yourself.

WHY SHOULD YOU DO NOTHING? WHAT ARE THE BENEFITS OF DOING NOTHING?

You become more relaxed as an individual by practicing the art of doing nothing.

The first reason doing nothing can actually be beneficial is this: You become more relaxed as an individual.

In Italy, they have a particular name for doing nothing: they call it *dolce far niente* (literally, the sweetness or joy of doing nothing). This phrase denotes a pleasant, sweet idleness. If you have absolutely no idea what the Italians mean by *dolce far niente*, you definitely need to take a trip to Italy to experience this concept for yourself.

If you lack the time, the means, or the opportunity to visit Italy (like I do), all hope is not lost. All you need to do is to watch *Eat Pray Love*, the 2010 movie starring Julia Roberts which is based on a 2006 memoir of the same name by Elizabeth Gilbert. Not only is this a fantastic movie that will clearly demonstrate to you the glorious idea of *dolce far niente*, but it will also serve to remind you of what your focus in life should be. The movie (or book, if you have time to read it) will serve to reorient you and help you place certain things in their proper perspective. This delightful movie helps to remind us all that merely operating as cogs in the factory machine or running around like a rat in a maze won't help to make us happier, healthier people. It asks you to take a breath, stop for a moment, and enjoy the beauty of life.

Eat Pray Love and the *dolce far niente* it depicts, rather than being a harbinger of utter moral degradation (as our 'always on, always working' society seems to imply), is instead a sweet and pleasant reminder of what's truly important in life. It offers a lovely balance to our collective modern mindset of basically working until we die.

Please don't get me wrong: Italians work. They work hard. In many cases, they work much harder than we do, live more difficult lives than we do, and suffer much more than we do on a daily basis. But that's why taking some time to do nothing, to practice *dolce far niente*, is so precious to them. They know how difficult life is, so they treasure each moment all the more and savor every breath, every taste, every sensation.

This doesn't mean you should do nothing for the rest of your life. Rather, it means that at least once in a while, you should take a break from your busy, hectic work life, relax, enjoy the sweetness of doing nothing, and remind yourself why you're actually alive and what you're living for.

Doing nothing will help with stress relief.

The second major benefit of doing nothing is that it relieves stress.

Believe it or not, there are several proven health benefits resulting from simply taking some time to relax. Stress from work (or any other facet of your life) takes an outsize and exceedingly negative toll on your body, and on your overall health. The stress hormones your body releases when you go through stressful situations will trigger your body's 'fight or flight' response.

Such a response is needed to protect you in the case of an emergency by preparing your body to react to the situation quickly. For instance, you'd certainly be thankful for your body's built-in fight or flight response if you were ever faced with a bear, staring a mountain lion in the face, or accosted by a mugger or attacker. However, other circumstances which will trigger the release of stress hormones include work pressure, project deadlines, or family situations. Since stressful situations now happen to us on a near-daily basis, many of us have an almost constant flood of stress hormones coursing through our veins. Unfortunately, because the human body wasn't designed to handle prolonged stress, this kind of continued stress response endangers our health.

What sort of health risks does one experience when under constant, chronic stress? At the very least, chronic stress can cause you to become irritable, experience anxiety, become increasingly depressed, be plagued with headaches, and/or suffer from insomnia. Other negative health effects from prolonged periods of stress may include heartburn, rapid breathing or hyperventilation, high blood pressure or hypertension, damaged blood vessels, a faster heartrate, an increased risk of stroke, an increased risk of heart disease, heart attacks, and other such cardiovascular incidents, high blood sugar (which can place you at a much higher risk for type 2 diabetes), osteoporosis, a weakened immune system, frequent stomach aches, problems with fertility in both men and women, erectile dysfunction, missed periods for women, a lowered sex drive for both men and women, tensed muscles (which lead to tension-related back pain, shoulder pain, headaches and body pain), overmedicating, overeating, weight gain, not eating enough, drug abuse, alcohol abuse, tobacco abuse, social withdrawal, nausea, vomiting, diarrhea, constipation, an increased risk of infection for the prostate and testes, a magnification of the physical symptoms of menopause, an increase in the amount of time the body needs in order to recover from an injury or illness, memory problems, and mental cloudiness (also known as brain fog).

Does all this sound scary? Well, it is. As you've likely determined from this downright terrifying list of health risks, prolonged stress leads both indirectly and directly to many leading causes of death. The modern workforce is suffering from a collective health problem, and that health problem is chronic stress.

So, sometimes it helps just to sit back and chill. (And no, I definitely don't mean chill and watch Netflix.) Take a moment to do nothing. Put down your phone, close your computer, and literally sit back and do nothing at all. For instance, you can close your eyes and just breathe deeply. Taking deep breaths for a few moments and clearing your mind in this manner will allow you to feel much better, no matter what's happening in your life or what you're going through. Spending some time to do nothing except take deep breaths has been shown to reduce stress levels significantly while promoting one's overall wellbeing.

Studies have also shown that practices like yoga and meditation have similar positive effects on your overall health and stress levels, but I fully understand that you may not want to do these things (or have time to do them). Yet every single one of us (and I mean every *single one of us*) has at least ten seconds in the day to pause, close our eyes, take several deep breaths, and do absolutely nothing. If you can learn to practice this at least once a day (but preferably several times a day), you'll do wonders for your stress levels and thus for your overall health and wellbeing. And if you can take even more time, say, fifteen minutes or even an hour, at some point in the day (perhaps in the middle of your otherwise busy workday or right after you get home), to simply do nothing—not to watch TV or be absorbed by your phone, but to actually lay aside all other things, sit down, close your eyes, and do *absolutely nothing*—this will undoubtedly reduce your levels of stress hormones even further.

Doing nothing is recommended by doctors.

Physicians always prescribe doing nothing as a remedy for just about every illness; they constantly tell you to 'Try to get plenty of rest'.

Any time you're feeling sick, this is the leitmotif you'll hear over and over again from your health professional. Your doctors will always tell you to do this, because they know all too well the myriad negative effects which chronic stress will exert on your health. By getting some rest, during which you're literally doing nothing productive whatsoever, you'll not only lower your stress levels but also give your body enough time to perform essential functions, such as allowing your cells to undergo the process of DNA repair—this involves fixing the damage done to your cells throughout the day through the normal metabolic process and your exposure to carcinogens and environmental factors like UV radiation. Damage to the DNA in our cells is a normal, everyday occurrence. However, this damage, when it fails to get repaired, is how our body develops cancer. If you want to reduce your stress levels (and thus reduce the various associated health risks) and give your body its best chance at avoiding cancer, you need to rest and do nothing.

So, take time to sit back, listen, and 'smell the coffee', as they say. Have a break, sit back, and unwind. This is literally one of the easiest things in the world for you to do. Resting, taking a break, and doing nothing takes literally no effort at all, but can make all the difference in the world when it comes to your health.

Doing nothing enables you to gather your thoughts and refresh your perspective.

Doing nothing also gives you the time to gather your thoughts, enabling you to obtain a refreshed perspective.

Taking a break allows you to compose yourself. Specifically, if you take your mind completely off whatever you're currently working on, when you come back to that task, you'll most likely receive fresh inspiration and a renewed take on the whole matter. Thus, taking a step back from whatever you're doing can truly improve your perspective on the task at hand, or give you the chance to regroup.

Sometimes, life, work, or the latest stressful situation can put us 'on the ropes'. So, one of the best things we can do for ourselves as individuals when faced with such a situation is to take a 'breather' every now and then and reassess our position on anything and everything. Moments such as these will drive us toward what our priorities ought to be, steering us toward the things that really matter.

So, take a breather once in a while. Do nothing for a few minutes. Give your brain and body a rest. Not only will you vastly improve your health, but you'll also improve your mental clarity and your ability to perform the task at hand.

Your performance will benefit from your taking a holiday.

Go on holiday.

Go ahead. Take a much-needed holiday. No matter how much stress your job may give you, and no matter how seemingly irreplaceable you may be, you can (and ought to) take holidays once in a while. If you're having difficulty remembering the last time you went on an actual holiday, you definitely need to take a holiday right away. Just do it. Take a day off (or a couple of days off) and use that to take a well-earned break. Seriously. If you can't remember the last time you took a holiday, you've probably worked long enough to accumulate several days off. Your team will be able to survive without you for a length of time.

And I don't mean a working holiday. Working holidays have their place, but this isn't what I'm talking about. In terms of lowering your stress levels and getting your body some much-needed rest so you can lower your risk of cancer and many other negative health effects, a working holiday will do you no good. Having your laptop and phone with you while you're on holiday so you're ready to respond to any sort of work crisis or request won't lower your stress levels or allow you to get the proper degree of rest.

If you're going to take a holiday, take an *actual* holiday. Take a break from work, and don't do anything, even if it's only for a day. Don't make this a super-active holiday where you're running around trying to see everything and meet everyone. Get some actual rest. Lower your stress levels. Your body will thank you. When you return from your holiday, you'll be well-rested and approach your work with renewed vigor and a fresh state of mind.

Doing nothing will help you avoid burnout.

Believe it or not, life's not all about 'doing'. If you think it is, you need some readjustment. Refer to the concept of *dolce far niente* that was discussed previously. You shouldn't be living to work; you should be working to live. A job will provide you with sustenance and fulfilment, but it shouldn't be the be-all and end-all of your very existence. In fact, overdoing things can and will lead to 'burnout' and can even cause long-term damage to your self-esteem. Unfortunately, throughout my career, I've seen this happen to people time and time again in both the private and public sector.

What exactly is burnout? It's a condition in which you experience physical, mental, and emotional exhaustion due to prolonged and excessive stress. You may be experiencing burnout right now without even realizing it. The stress caused by the inability to meet the constant demands of your job can cause you to become emotionally and mentally drained. Continued stress may cause you to lose the motivation and interest which directed you to assume that responsibility in the first place.

Burnout causes your productivity to diminish and saps your energy, leaving you with increased feelings of hopelessness, helplessness, cynicism, and resentment. You may eventually feel like you've been utterly consumed and there's nothing more you can give.

The detrimental effects of burnout will take their toll on every area of your life—your work life, your social life and your home life. The condition of being burned out can also result in long-term negative changes to the body, making you more vulnerable to everyday illnesses such as the flu or the common cold and increasing your risk of several other more serious illnesses. Due to the many consequences of burnout, it's vital that you deal with this condition right away.

Allow me to illustrate this with an example. A few years ago, I had an exceedingly talented colleague at work. Every outward indicator pointed to his lasting success in our company. He was going to take us forward and make us better and more successful than we'd ever been before. Due to his obvious aptitude, the boss gave him several projects to work on at the same time. He was made the head of two teams that were responsible for two group projects, as well as being given a few individual projects to complete. And he could do it. In fact, he actually did it. He didn't get a whole lot of sleep and he'd often forget to eat proper meals unless the team he was heading up ordered food, but he managed to pull off all of these projects with aplomb. Our organization certainly benefited at that time from his amazing work, which he undertook at a feverish, unprecedented pace over the course of four months.

But you know what? After four months of working at the company (during which he was actually able to complete all those work projects), he suffered a stroke. An actual stroke. At the age of twenty-seven! The blood flow to his brain was compromised, and he was never the same again. He was unable even to walk and to talk normally, let alone accomplish the difficult tasks he'd been able to accomplish with relative ease before. Were those four months of work worth his lifelong health and brain function? Absolutely not!

Okay, so that was an extreme example. But I can assure you that his was by no means the only case of severe burnout I've seen in my time. I've seen coworkers descend into deep bouts of clinical depression, attempt to kill themselves (and even succeed in doing so, regrettably), and develop all manner of problems in their work life, home life, and social life due to burnout. In addition, I've seen several other promising employees get so burned out that, although they didn't suffer from any immediate or apparent physical effects, they became so utterly disenchanted with their work that they prematurely left what could have been extremely successful careers.

Believe me. You need to take this seriously. You may not actually have a stroke or a heart attack while you're on the job, or drop dead as a result of burnout during a staff meeting, but it will exert a very real toll on your overall health, your wellbeing and your relationships with others, whether you see it or not. And even if burnout doesn't actually kill you or debilitate you while you're on the job, it will certainly shorten your lifespan and bring you closer to death. Is that worthwhile? I think not.

The talented young man from the example could've taken fewer projects at once and accomplished them over a longer period, allowing him to sleep and eat properly while reducing his blood pressure and overall stress levels. He could've accomplished fifty or 500 projects with the company instead of just five. Doing those five projects in such a short timespan was by no means worth his entire working life and career. If he'd worked at a slower pace and not stressed himself out so much, he could've not only preserved his health and his quality of life, but also had a spectacularly rich, fulfilling, and long career, adding untold value to his organization.

When it comes to burnout, nobody wins. Not the burned-out individual, and not the organization they work for. It's simply not a sound life or business practice to become burned out or let your employees become burned out. After all, even if you remove the tragic human component of the equation and look at this from purely a business perspective, if talented (or at least competent and productive) employees keep getting burned out, their level of productivity drops significantly or the business has to invest significant resources to keep retraining new employees. If this coworker of mine hadn't been burned out and suffered that stroke, he could've done fantastic work and had an amazing career, and the organization could've been taken to new heights as well.

Be proactive about doing nothing.

When you're working on a challenging project, take some time to do nothing. As soon as you stop working on your project and start doing nothing, through the principle of inertia, your brain will remain busy and rearrange the puzzle pieces in your mind, bestowing on you a much broader perspective on the task at hand—and indeed on life itself. This can allow you not only to gain a fresh perspective on your work project and approach it with new light and inspiration, but also help you regain control over your life.

I'm sure we've all encountered this at one point or another in our lives; we just need to be reminded of this fact. When I'm working on a difficult project or challenging task, if I'm stuck, usually all I need to do in order to get my creative juices flowing again is to sleep on it. I go to sleep and make sure that the last thing I think about before falling asleep is the project, allowing my subconscious to put the puzzle pieces together for me while I'm asleep. In the morning, nine times out of ten I wake up with the exact knowledge of how to solve the problem or continue with my task. Writers experience this too. Ever heard of writer's block? I obviously haven't personally interviewed every single writer who's ever lived, but when it comes to my writer friends, none of them say that the way to get over writer's block is to keep staring at that blinking line in your word processor. Almost all of them say that the best way to get over writer's block is to take your mind completely off what you're writing and do something else for a little while.

So, the next time you're stuck on something or feel like you're moving more slowly than you should be, don't try to forge ahead and keep doing what you've been doing. Change it up. Take a break and try doing nothing for a little while. Take a walk around the building or neighborhood and empty your mind of anything related to that project. Or just sleep on it. Pushing the pause button and doing nothing for a little while can work wonders for your freshness, vitality, and productivity when you return to the task.

Doing nothing can rearrange certain matters in your life.

Sometimes, doing nothing can help you rearrange things. Taking a breather from whatever you're doing will allow you to become reoriented and gain a fresh perspective on life in general. As I said earlier, a movie like *Eat Pray Love* can help you realize what's truly important in life. Doing nothing for a short and sweet period will allow you to take stock of what you've accomplished in your career and life, giving you the time and opportunity to reset your priorities and reconfigure them if necessary. Remember that you shouldn't live to work, but work to live. Your career isn't the purpose of your existence, and if it is, you need some serious readjustment.

After all, nobody on their deathbed says, 'I wish I'd spent more time in the office'. Instead, that person says, 'I wish I'd spent more time with my family', or 'I wish I'd spent more time appreciating the simpler things in life'. Regret isn't a good feeling —so save yourself the heartache of regret by taking a break from what you're doing and remind yourself what truly matters in your life.

Addressing the concern of potential procrastination, it's essential to acknowledge objections to inaction and provide thoughtful responses. The first objection centers on the idea that doing nothing may result in procrastination.

Doing nothing will lead to procrastination and a complete lack of productivity *only* if you continue doing nothing for an extended period. It wouldn't be wise, for instance, to do nothing for the entire day and waste your entire workday.

As we know, one of the major benefits of doing nothing is that it gives your brain and subconscious time to refocus and reconfigure, allowing you to return to the task at hand with renewed vigor and inspiration. But to get this refreshed brain and renewed inspiration, you must return to the task at hand.

Thus, taking occasional breaks to lower your stress levels and reassess yourself is perfectly fine, but if you take too much time doing this, you may end up becoming a victim of procrastination. You may fail to accomplish the tasks which have been set for you, elevating your stress levels due to being fired and not being able to sustain yourself and your family.

So, it's perfectly fine and healthy to take some breaks throughout the day and do nothing for short periods, but don't overdo it. Don't go for a holiday while you're on the job. If you're on the job, be on the job. And if you're on holiday, be on holiday. Don't mix the two and try to take an eight-hour holiday by doing nothing during your workday.

Addressing the concern of low self-esteem, it's important to recognize that taking no action may contribute to a decline in one's self-worth.

It's true that doing nothing in a habitual manner or for extended periods (during the times you're supposed to be doing something) can lead to low self-esteem for some. However, this problem's easily solved: Don't do nothing all the time. Be selective, discerning, and judicious about the breaks you take and the times you spend doing nothing. The goal of doing nothing is to become more relaxed, reduce your stress levels, elevate your overall level of health and wellbeing, remind you what truly matters in life, refresh your perspective, and make you more productive and clearer-minded when you're working. Just be smart about it. Work when you need to work and rest when you need to rest. Taking a minute or so every hour to close your eyes, take some deep breaths, and do absolutely nothing certainly won't lower your level of self-esteem. Quite the contrary, in fact. After such an invigorating break, you'll be able to return to your work with fresh eyes and will be even more productive than you were before, thus elevating your self-esteem and raising your level of self-fulfillment.

Of course, there are certain people who find immediately that they don't in fact need to do anything to maintain their self-esteem; they suffer not one bit from the low self-esteem that's supposed to come with prolonged periods of doing nothing, and instead remain wholly satisfied with the way their life is shaped during these times.

The major issue with this type of person is that they're inhibited from growing and evolving, whether mentally, professionally, spiritually or individually.

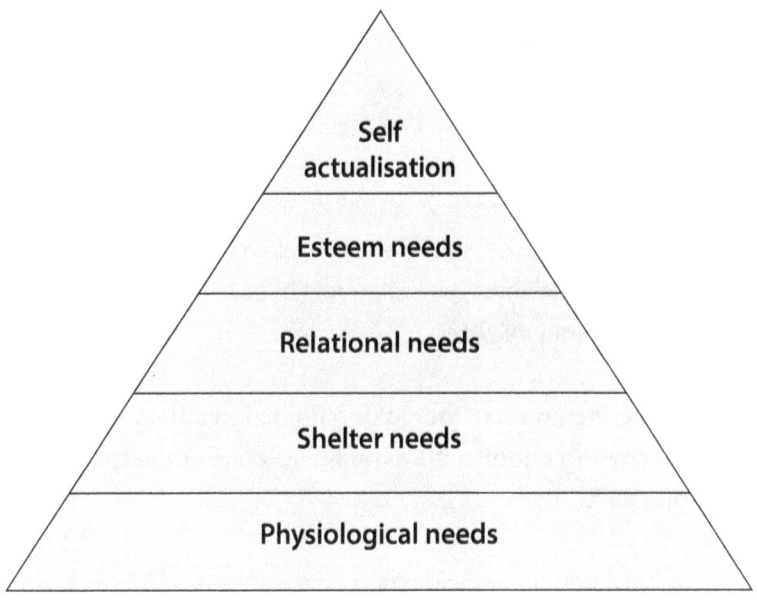

Consider Maslow's hierarchy of needs. His five-tier model of human needs, frequently depicted as a pyramid, has physiological needs like food, water, warmth, and rest at the base. One level above that are the needs related to personal security and safety. And above that, we have the needs of love and belonging, involving friends and intimate relationships. The fourth level of the pyramidal hierarchy involves the needs related to one's self-esteem, such as feelings of accomplishment and prestige. The fifth and highest level (and consequently the hardest one to get to in human life) is self-actualization, which involves achieving one's full potential.

The person who never suffers from low self-esteem after doing nothing all the time is forever stopped at the fourth level, and is never able to reach the level of self-actualization. Why? Because self-actualization involves *doing something*. So, if you never do anything in life, you'll never achieve your full potential.

Don't do nothing all the time. Practice doing nothing when it's necessary, such as when you're feeling overly stressed out, blocked, or burned out. Your practice of doing nothing should make you fresher and more successful when you return to doing something, so that you can achieve your full potential as a person and reach the level of self-actualization.

Addressing the concern that taking no action ultimately results in life becoming chaotic, it's essential to consider responses to this objection.

It's true that if you do nothing all the time, every day, you may end up living in your own little reality, a bubble of sorts, with no proper perspective on life.

For instance, if all you do is sleep all day long, sit on the couch and drool, or watch Netflix all day and all night, you'll soon lose track of the time (literally—you won't know what day or time it is, or even how many hours have passed) and begin to lose your grip on reality. Really, there's nothing worse than this.

So, don't let this happen to you. Don't do nothing all the time. Develop a plan. *Any* plan. Even if it doesn't seem like such a good plan to you, what matters is that you have a plan. Once you have a plan, it can always be improved.

DOING NOTHING—THE BOTTOM LINE

The concept of 'doing nothing' has gotten an admittedly bad rap in modern society.

In many societies of the modern world, people promote a 'pull yourself up by the bootstraps', rags to riches, always-on work culture that looks down on spending time doing absolutely nothing. However, this sort of 'sped up', twenty-four-hour workday culture has had vastly detrimental effects on the health and the wellbeing of Americans by giving us nearly constant levels of stress and causing us to become burned out. Stress and burnout, in turn, take an incalculable negative toll on our health, self-esteem, mental state, familial relationships, and overall wellbeing.

Thus, taking a break occasionally to do absolutely nothing (by sitting down, closing your eyes, and taking some deep breaths, for example), can work wonders when it comes to your mood, physical health, mental state, self-esteem, and productivity. Such timely breaks, as well as a newfound awareness of the concept of *dolce far niente*, will not only make you healthier, give you a fresh mind, and cause you to be more productive, but also give you the time and opportunity to take stock of your life and gain a fresh perspective on what's truly important.

But don't overdo it, because if you spend too much time doing nothing, it may lead to procrastination as well as low self-esteem.

Remember, everything in moderation! Don't take the concept of doing nothing and utilize it to an extreme. If you do nothing twenty-four hours a day for the rest of your life (or for an extended period when you're supposed to be working), this can also prove detrimental to your health by leading to procrastination (and the excessive stress which accompanies it), low self-esteem (from not achieving the fourth and fifth level of Maslow's hierarchy of needs), and more health problems (from the severe stress caused by losing your job and thus your source of income and livelihood).

As we dig further into the details of maximizing the benefits of seemingly unproductive moments, our journey doesn't end here. The forthcoming chapter unveils an additional reward associated with mastering the art of intentional inactivity.

To unravel this hidden advantage and discover how it can be harnessed in your favor, let's seamlessly transition into the next chapter. Keep reading to explore the nuanced dynamics of leveraging idleness for strategic gains.

CHAPTER 4

HOW TO DO NOTHING AND GET PROMOTED

Procrastination is a sign of a perfectionist.

— PATRICK J KENNEDY

In this chapter, I'll be walking you through several examples of ways certain people get promoted—not necessarily by doing nothing at all, but rather by doing nothing in comparison to others such as their peers or team members.

WHAT EXACTLY DOES IT MEAN TO DO NOTHING AND GET PROMOTED?

In the previous chapter, we explored the concept of doing nothing and relayed the various benefits of this practice, which range from health benefits to career benefits to overall benefits in life. However, this chapter contains information about utilizing the practice of doing nothing in the extreme.

In this case, I'm not talking about simply taking occasional breaks to sit back, relax, breathe deeply, and reorient yourself to get a clear head. I'm talking about the people who do basically nothing all day long and add no value at all to their organization.

I'm speaking of those who choose to sit back and let their peers and fellow employees do all the work, then step in and receive all the glory and success, resulting in their being promoted undeservedly when in reality it was the other employees or team members who did the work on the projects and deserved the promotion. Unfortunately, the fact that this individual contributed nothing to the project allowed them a strategic opportunity to take advantage of the ones who were doing the work.

There's a somewhat less negative possibility when it comes to 'doing nothing and getting promoted'. In addition to those who do nothing in comparison to their peers and manage to get promoted anyway, there are other individuals who do nothing most of the time, so it seems like they're always doing nothing. However, these folks are the type of people who do some of their best work under pressure. That is, by procrastinating and doing nothing for most of the time (and projecting the image to others that nothing's being done), these people get quite a bit done once they start to work, causing them to be more productive in a much shorter amount of time and resulting in their promotion.

In such cases, the promotion or advancement may not be undeserved and earned on the backs of the other people. Rather, other people may not believe that the individual deserves that promotion because although they've done the necessary work to deserve it, fellow employees barely ever see that individual working. This is because they procrastinate most of the time and finish the work in a speedy and unseen manner right before the deadline, leading to the general impression that they're basically doing nothing.

So, in the context of this chapter, the idea of doing nothing includes not only the version of doing nothing from Chapter 3 but also the concept of doing nothing when applied in the extreme (and when used to the detriment of others) in addition to the concept of projecting the image or impression that one's doing nothing, yet being quite successful once they begin to work.

WHY DO PEOPLE DO NOTHING AND STILL GET PROMOTED? HOW DO THEY BENEFIT FROM DOING NOTHING?

They can tie themselves to others' success.

To get promoted by doing nothing, you first need to tie yourself to the success of others.

Unfortunately, I've seen this happen far too often, both in the private and the public sector. I call these people 'leeches', in the sense that such people are parasitic and always tie themselves to other people's successes and hard work. A leech is a freeloader who sucks the blood of another organism without providing anything in return; a parasitic relationship is one in which one person benefits at the expense of another.

There are three kinds of relationships in this sense of the word: mutualistic relationships, communalistic relationships, and parasitic relationships.

- A **mutualistic relationship** is one in which both parties derive mutual benefit or gain from one another.
- A **communalistic relationship** is one in which one party derives benefit or gain from the other, and the other party derives neither gain nor harm from the relationship.
- A **parasitic relationship** is one in which one party derives benefit or gain from the other party by sticking to the other party and causing them harm.

Don't be fooled by those who do nothing while tying themselves to the successes of other people and get promoted by doing so. Such a person is a leech, a parasite. That individual is not in a mutualistic or communalist relationship of any kind. The individual might not seem to be actively harming other people, but mark my words: Harm's being done. When that person hitches their wagon to another person's rising star, they serve only to slow the star down and impede the progress that could've been made.

Unfortunately, this strategy works more often than I would care to admit. Several people have become CEOs and top managers in various organizations not due to their hard work, but simply because they were able to link their own persona to the successful work of others.

They are more rested and thus more able to spot opportunities.

Believe it or not, people who do nothing can get promoted because they're more ... well-rested.

Some people will take full advantage of their coworker's skills in a negative way. Since these leeches are doing nothing, they're able to collect on the benefits resulting from the hard work done by others. They tend to let their colleagues do all the heavy lifting and simply reap the rewards. The people from whom these leeches steal the credit are simply too tired, stressed out, or burned out to even notice that the credit which should rightfully go to them is being stolen.

Consider the hypothetical example of two people who are walking up to a house at the top of a steep hill to attend a party. They're tasked with pushing a man in a wheelchair up to the entrance (probably since all the parking spaces which should've been reserved for those who are handicapped have been taken up by perfectly able-bodied people). However, of the two people, only one is pushing the man in the wheelchair up the hill. The other person is simply walking to the side of the wheelchair and doesn't lift a finger to help. Once the three people arrive at the top of the hill, the person who's been pushing the man in the wheelchair the entire way pauses for a minute or two to lean against a tree or a wall to catch his breath and mop the sweat from his brow. In that instant, the other able-bodied person who didn't help at all in pushing the man in the wheelchair up the hill but merely walked alongside them is standing next to the wheelchair. He sees the host of the gathering (who resides in the house) walking toward the man in the wheelchair. At that instant, the man who did nothing chooses calculatingly to place his hands on the handles of the wheelchair, and the host greets him and thanks him profusely for going to all the trouble of pushing the man in the wheelchair all the way up the hill. In the meantime, the person who pushed the wheelchair stands by, aghast, but too out of breath and exhausted to speak up for himself.

Because the man who did no wheelchair pushing whatsoever was well-rested, he was able to spot an opportunity to gain the credit and engender his own advancement and goodwill on the back of another.

I understand that your work situation may not correspond exactly to this hypothetical one, but you get my point. By doing nothing, a person is more well-rested and in a better condition to take advantage of the hard work done by others for their own parasitic advancement.

They're more relaxed.

Doing nothing can get you promoted because you're more ... relaxed.

This is directly related to the point above about being more well-rested. As strange as this may seem, doing nothing places you in opposition to your peers, which means that while they're involved in the 'nitty gritty' of things, you retain a clearer, more focused mind, and are thus actually able to spot opportunities for advancement better and faster than your coworker. While your fellow employees are busy creating the successes and putting in the hard work for which you'll eventually take credit, simply because you've positioned yourself as a 'team leader' and a more clear-headed decision maker, you'll spot the opportunities for your promotion and advancement within the organization.

They're sometimes more efficient.

Doing nothing causes you to seek out efficiency. Sometimes (or is it more accurate to say, all the time?), this is what's in the mind of a leader. Leaders, from my experience, always care about finding the most efficient way to do something. This also implies the act of doing nothing, by the way, since you're delegating your tasks to others in the organization. Some managers and leaders delegate the heck out of their tasks to the interns who work for them, or to the team members they trust. These leaders or managers are there to check up on those to whom they've assigned the tasks, but once the process is in place and running well, it's usually smooth sailing from there.

In a nutshell, managers seek to be as efficient as they can possibly be, and one foundational premise of being efficient is to take as little time as possible to do something. Doing nothing is inherent to this concept, since you're left with extra time on your hands (after finishing the task assigned in as little time as possible) during which you're probably free to do nothing.

They have time to take a step back and examine the big picture.

Doing nothing allows you to fully realize the consequences and ramifications of every decision or project. As your team or colleagues are busy working their way through their tasks, you're free to foresee all the consequences, meaning that you have the time to carefully consider what will happen if things go well, or go south. This opportunity for foresight when it comes to the consequences of decisions, projects, and assignments at work enables you to make decisions and voice opinions which are seemingly smarter and more beneficial than those of your peers, simply because they've been doing all the work and haven't had the time to make such thorough considerations.

These wise decisions and opinions regarding the consequences you've had time to consider will go a long way toward getting you promoted and helping you advance in your organization while the rest of your coworkers are busy doing the actual work which has been assigned to them.

According to psychologist Avigail Lev, we often tend to assume procrastination inherently leads to failure. However, some people can complete their tasks right before the deadline, so they're just more successful that way.

AN ALTERNATIVE POINT OF VIEW

Procrastination can get you promoted, if used correctly. This is because, if nothing else, the act of procrastination somewhat counterintuitively helps you learn to manage your time better and become more efficient when you need to work from time to time.

HOW DO PEOPLE DO NOTHING AND GET PROMOTED? WHAT ARE SOME BENEFITS AND DRAWBACKS?

Rely on others to keep you accountable.

If you involve some of the other people around you, you'll be able to fight the condition of doing nothing in the extreme (that is, doing nothing at work for days or weeks on end). Since this is likely to be detrimental to your career (especially if your boss gets wind of the fact that you're literally doing nothing), if you're naturally prone to such behavior, you should rely on the assistance of the others around you to keep yourself accountable. Seek the assistance of people you trust to nag you about meeting your own goals and deadlines. Make them hold you accountable for cutting short your times of doing nothing to keep this practice from exerting a negative toll on your career.

For instance, if you know you're prone to succumbing to sustained periods of doing nothing, you can enlist the help of your coworkers or team members to keep you on task. I knew an employee who was exceedingly absent-minded—his mind often wandered during staff meetings (causing him to be caught like a deer in the headlights and freeze open-mouthed whenever his boss or a fellow employee would ask him a question) and during the regular workday. However, the work that he did was of a decent quality, so his bosses put up with his absent-minded shenanigans for a while.

However, things eventually came to a head. One day, he missed a deadline for a particular project entirely. He didn't just miss the deadline—he forgot to even *begin* the task which had been assigned to him. Obviously, this behavior was utterly unacceptable. However, his bosses had some mercy on him and allowed him to continue his employment in the organization (but with a warning and a demotion).

To prevent himself from ever committing the same error again, he enlisted his coworkers' assistance. Specifically, he asked colleagues in the three adjacent cubicles to keep him accountable for the tasks to which he was assigned. His boss always assigned tasks to him verbally, so whenever his boss told him to do something, all three coworkers would hear the task and make a mental note of it.

The three coworkers took turns to check on him and nag him as needed. The one directly across the aisle would simply spin around in her chair to check on him briefly and give him a stern word to get his head out of the clouds if she saw him daydreaming or doing something other than the task which had been assigned to him. The two coworkers to his right and left checked on him less frequently, but every so often they would stand up and peek over their cubicle walls to see if he was doing what he was supposed to. If they found him slacking, they'd pelt him with Nerf foam footballs to snap him out of his daydream. (To be honest, they sometimes bombarded him with Nerf footballs even when he was doing what he was supposed to be doing, but that's beside the point.) And to make doubly sure he never missed another deadline, all three of them would remind him once every thirty minutes that he had a project due when the deadline was a day or two away. (They couldn't do very much to help him with his inattentiveness during staff meetings, but he figured out his own methods to keep himself attentive and his head out of the clouds at those times.)

Through asking the people around him to keep him accountable, he kept himself from falling into old patterns and committing past errors. That way, even if they caught him doing nothing, he was soon shaken out of that condition to return to a more productive mode. Also, because he enlisted the help of his coworkers, they felt responsible for him. His successes became their successes in the best way possible, since they had effectively enabled him to achieve those successes.

Procrastination can make a certain type of person more efficient.

Honestly, some people simply function better when they procrastinate. You may be this type of person (or you may instead be marveling that such a type of person even exists). These people are simply not efficient at all when it comes to working, unless they're within shouting distance of the deadline. When the deadline's far away and they have more than enough time to accomplish the task assigned to them, they do nothing (or just about everything except what they're supposed to be doing), and they while away the time until the deadline draws frighteningly near, at which point they *finally* begin working and finish the project in record time with aplomb.

Even if they try to start working on the project well before the deadline, they find themselves working at a mind-numbingly slow pace. They may even wonder what's wrong with them, since they're so capable of finishing tasks at a high speed when the deadline's nearly upon them, but they can't manage to maintain even a reasonable speed when the deadline's far away.

Work, for these people, progresses at a snail's pace until a few days (or even perhaps a few hours) before the deadline arrives, and then the work progresses at an astounding and near-superhuman rate so that they finish right on time.

These people simply work better under pressure. A friend of mine who owns a successful company told me that he prefers to procrastinate, simply because he loves to make decisions under pressure, and also loves the adrenaline rush of accomplishing what he needs to do in as short a time as possible. The fact that the deadline's so near gives him adequate pressure to do an excellent job, and that pressure triggers in him a fight or flight response which allows him to run his company successfully. Accomplishing what he needs to do in as little time as humanly possible not only supplies him with that adrenaline rush, but also gives him a sense of accomplishment and the feeling that no-one else in the organization (or on Earth, frankly) could have done as good a job as he did in as short an amount of time.

And he may be right.

If you're one of those people who work better under pressure and are made more efficient through procrastinating, then doing nothing—when the deadline for your assignment's still far away—may be an effective use of your time. You can use that time to relax and lower your stress levels, especially when they'll be elevated as the deadline draws near and you need to start doing something. But, hey, if it works for you, then it works. Find out what works for you and allows you to accomplish the highest quality of work. This will put you on the best path for promotion and advancement, no matter what conditions you work best under.

Doing nothing can make you more productive.

There's another category of those who 'do nothing'. I know some individuals who are more productive at their work precisely because they use a lot of their time seemingly 'doing nothing' for their company, but who are using that time to do things they enjoy.

This may seem decidedly counterintuitive, but for these individuals, this is their way of giving back to the company. By spending time doing a host of other things they enjoy doing, they become much more productive, enlightened, and fulfilled when performing the tasks which have been assigned to them. And taking the time to do the things they enjoy gives them inspiration, which they then apply to add value to their organization.

This is a genuine concept. Google (or its parent company, Alphabet), which routinely makes *Fortune*'s list of the one hundred best companies in the world to work for, believes strongly in this philosophy—that when employees are surrounded by things they enjoy doing and an overwhelmingly positive work atmosphere, they'll become more productive, more creative, and add more value to the company. Therefore, Google offers a high degree of flexibility to its employees, allowing them to set their own schedules, arrive to work late or go home early if they need to, and work from home if they want. It's also the reason why the Google campus (also known as the Googleplex) is filled with foosball tables, nap pods, gaming rooms, and numerous other amusements and amenities making it more akin to an amusement park than a high-powered tech company. Employees can also eat a gourmet breakfast, lunch, and dinner at the Googleplex, and can even sleep at the office in comfortable accommodation if they'd like. Google's goal in providing such an environment for its workers is to make them the happiest, healthiest, and most productive employees in the world.

Google has tapped into the thought that if an employee is healthy, happy, and relaxed, they'll work better and be more inspired, creative, and productive than if they were stressed out or gloomy. All the things that would normally be considered a distraction in the workplace (such as foosball tables, arcade games, swimming pools, billiards, ping pong tables, video games and designated napping rooms with nap pods) are not only present at the Google campus, but even encouraged.

And it's not as if Google accepts constant procrastination and everyone doing nothing and playing games all the time. They expect high-quality work. My friend who works for Google tells me that before he gets to code something up for work, he must lay out all the groundwork, writing up design flows, consulting with other coders, and getting everything approved before he can get to the actual coding. Google's not a company that accepts shoddy or half-baked work. (It certainly didn't get to be one of the biggest companies in the world that way.) But the point is that Google trusts its employees to get the job done and provides them with all the entertainment, amusements, and sustenance they may need to achieve their goals.

And that's not all. The employees of Google are encouraged by the company to pursue their own dreams and pet projects while on the company's dime. They can use their working hours to explore their own ideas and code them up. Google literally pays them to do their own thing. And you know what? Several of the best, most popular Google products came out of such pet projects.

Do you see what I mean when I say that these types of employees add value and give back to the organization they work for by doing the things they enjoy, other than the task which has been directly assigned to them? In such a case, 'doing nothing' can make you more productive because although you may not be working on the project assigned to you, the things you're doing still add value to the company because you do them with fervor and passion. And they allow you to reduce your stress levels, become more relaxed and inspired, and return with fresh eyes to your assigned work, making you more productive, efficient, and insightful.

Now that's what I call 'doing nothing and getting promoted'. If you can do that, then that promotion is surely well-deserved. I just hope your bosses see the light and give you what you deserve instead of treating you like a derelict, do-nothing employee.

NOW, LET'S LOOK AT SOME OBJECTIONS TO DOING NOTHING AND GETTING PROMOTED, AND THE RESPONSES TO THOSE OBJECTIONS.

While some may object, arguing that linking one's success to others is unethical, it's essential to consider alternative perspectives on the matter.

It's indeed unethical and immoral to link your success to others—but if it gets you where you want to be and helps you to achieve advancement in your organization without any hard work or effort, do you really care? You'll undoubtedly follow your own goals and aspirations (especially if you're seeking to be one of these immoral employees who obtains success by stabbing others in the back).

While striving for a promotion, relying on inactivity as a strategy is unsustainable in the long run. Eventually, you risk facing exclusion or being exposed.

From my experience, several employees who practice this strategy are still hanging on, so it depends on how good you are at executing this tactic. If you treat it as a game, you may be surprised at the results.

Addressing procrastination is crucial for personal development, and it's essential to eradicate it from your life to enhance overall wellbeing and productivity.

Despite what you've been trained by your elementary school teachers to believe, procrastination isn't that bad at all. It can be an exceedingly effective advancement strategy, one which you can choose deliberately to make yourself more efficient and productive while advancing your own objectives.

DOING NOTHING AND GETTING PROMOTED—THE BOTTOM LINE

If you link yourself to the success of others, it's entirely possible to do nothing and get promoted.

It's indeed possible to do basically nothing in comparison to your peers while still getting promoted and advancing far above them. The key to accomplishing this is linking yourself to the success and hard work of your coworker (and possibly even that of your boss). Doing so will allow you to look good to your superiors and be promoted with the least amount of effort. It may be a snake-like move, but it works if you want to go down that path.

Doing nothing may actually cause you to become even *more* efficient and skilled at allocating your time.

Also, don't look down on procrastination. It can be a very effective and useful tool (if you're wired that way). Doing nothing for most of your time can make you much more efficient at allocating your time wisely and much more productive when you begin your work.

Doing nothing will allow you to better spot and take advantage of opportunities for advancement.

Another lesson to learn in the implementation of the strategy of doing nothing and managing to get promoted is that by doing nothing, you'll place yourself in a better condition (both mentally and physically) to spot advancement opportunities more quickly and to seize them accordingly.

CHAPTER 5
HOW TO BE SAFE

Being busy is not the same as being productive.

— TIM FERRISS

In this chapter, I'll be discussing the idea of how you as an employee can 'stay safe' at work, why this practice is the best course of action for you to pursue, and why it's advisable for you to act in such a manner.

WHAT DOES IT MEAN TO BE SAFE?

In the context of this chapter, 'being safe' or 'staying safe' refers to the practice of creating a safe and stable work environment for yourself. The ideal environment is one in which you don't become embroiled in office politics or any disputes with your coworker, and in which you maintain reasonable expectations and a set of goals and achievements which are actually feasible and attainable for you and can be maintained over a long period for the sake of your career.

Let's break down each aspect of staying safe in more detail.

Staying safe, when it comes to your relationships with your fellow coworker, means staying out of any interoffice disputes between employees, remaining neutral when becoming involved is unavoidable, staying completely unbiased by listening to both sides of the argument when you must be involved, and practicing empathy whenever you're dealing with your fellow coworker so they're able to trust you and make you their confidant.

Staying safe, when it comes to the workload assigned to you and the tasks for which you're responsible, is crucial to consistently appearing busy while projecting an active and engaged demeanor. This strategic approach aims to convey dedication and competence to colleagues and superiors, fostering a positive perception of your work ethic within the professional sphere.

Looking busy will prevent your boss or your coworker from dumping a ton of extra work on you. Your boss and your coworker will also be much less likely to bother you with trivial and unimportant matters.

Please note that staying safe doesn't involve completing the work you're assigned in a sloppy manner. To stay safe, you must do the work you're assigned, and do it well. Just don't complete it so quickly that your boss elevates their expectations of you to an unreasonable (and eventually unattainable) level.

So, staying safe involves doing the tasks you're assigned in a proper manner and looking busy all the time.

WHY SHOULD YOU TRY TO BE SAFE? WHAT ARE THE BENEFITS OF BEING SAFE?

You can impress your boss.

If you can become adept at making yourself 'look busy', you'll likely end up making a good impression on your boss or your bosses, which can engender the idea that you're a hard worker.

According to Melanie Curtin of *Inc. Magazine*, research suggests that in an eight-hour day, the average worker is only productive for two hours and fifty-three minutes. Because many of us work for fewer than three hours out of a possible eight, you don't even need to push yourself too hard to look busy and project to your superiors the thought that you're a person who works hard and deserves promotion and advancement.

You can stay out of office conflict and office politics.

If you look busy all the time, you'll be spared from most office conflicts. Each office or place of business has its own congregations or parties; if you find yourself on one side, you automatically antagonize the other person or people. So, one of the best ways to stay safe at work is to focus on your own tasks, mind your own business, collaborate when necessary, and help others when they need help or ask you for it. Don't choose sides or get pulled into any interoffice disputes or complicated workplace politics. That's pretty much it.

You can maintain neutrality and protect yourself from gossip.

Emulate Switzerland. Be neutral. No matter what the subject is or who the people involved are, stay neutral and unbiased. Focus on what you must do and let the others in your workplace do what they have to do. Offer them assistance if they require it, and stay away from people who gossip a lot, or risk becoming a subject of gossip yourself. Staying neutral, avoiding gossip, and being unbiased toward all your coworkers by treating them equally is a key component of elevating your degree of safety and popularity in the workplace.

Show empathy to others in order to stay safe.

Don't pry. Instead, show empathy. If you become known as an empathetic person and you engender trust in others, coworkers will feel free to share their worries and problems with you. You can become the confidant of your coworkers. Value their trust and allow them to talk to you. Don't consider them a nuisance; in most cases, they'll provide their own solutions to the challenges they're encountering, but you'll have provided them with an avenue for doing so by allowing them to talk through the matter with you. As a result, you'll increase their respect and trust for you, enhancing your level of workplace safety.

You can keep yourself from receiving additional workloads.

Here's one that may sound a bit self-serving: You'll be able to stay safe if you look busy because you won't have to complete the tasks of the other employees who may work more slowly than you.

Let's say you've managed to finish all your work in much less than the allotted time. I'd advise you not to notify your boss, your superior, or your fellow coworker of the fact that you're done with your work too early on. If you tell your boss or peers that you're finished, your boss may assign you another more difficult task or order you to help finish the work that your peers have yet to complete.

So, go easy on the enthusiasm and ardor—such excessive enthusiasm could very well result in several additional workloads for you, which can in turn result in higher stress levels and burnout, which, as I discussed earlier, can be exceedingly detrimental to your health and overall wellbeing.

AN ALTERNATIVE POINT OF VIEW

I'm busy looking busy because I've done my work and I don't want to do yours. This may be the mindset of someone who practices looking busy and staying safe. They don't want to be saddled with the extra unfinished work of their coworker.

HOW CAN YOU PRACTICE STAYING SAFE? WHAT ARE SOME SCENARIOS YOU CAN WORK WITH?

Avoid gossip at all costs.

Never stick around if you notice that your coworkers are starting to gossip. Excuse yourself from the situation by saying something along the lines of 'I have a meeting' or 'My phone is ringing' or 'I have to get back to work on that project', etc., and seize that opportunity to walk away. Don't look back. Don't subject yourself to hearing any type of office gossip. And *don't* actively participate in office gossip. This is by far the smartest choice in the long run.

Those who spread and participate in office gossip, however passively they may be doing it, are doomed to incite discord and ill will throughout their workplace, ultimately damaging their careers and creating a toxic work environment.

Unfortunately, when it comes to gossip, it's all too common that the person or people gossiping soon become the ones about whom *others* gossip. If you never participate in office gossip of any kind, then you won't, for instance, overhear the rumor one coworker's spreading about another (who happens to be your friend), and be put in an awkward situation where you're forced to take sides. If you never hear or participate in the gossip relating to interoffice politics and/or who got which position for what reason, then you'll never have any reason to doubt the capabilities of your fellow employees, allowing you to trust them more (which in turn causes them to trust *you* more and builds an atmosphere of mutual respect). In addition, your coworker will eventually come to realize that you never participate in office gossip of any kind, and they'll confide in you more when it comes to their own personal or work-related problems or struggles.

I've had a great deal of personal experience in this matter. Several years ago, when I began working at the company where I remain employed to this day, I resolved never to partake in any sort of office gossip (even if it seemed like harmless water cooler talk). I made this resolution because I'd been somewhat affected by gossip at my previous workplace, and I didn't want to engender that kind of situation again. I'd always walk away (or sometimes even run away) if I received the faintest hint that my fellow employees were beginning to gossip. I became known as the no-nonsense, gossip-free person. In fact, after I'd practiced this for a few weeks, whenever I walked around the office, if people had been gossiping, they stopped as soon as they saw me coming. They knew that I'd have no part in that sort of nonsense, so they stopped immediately whenever they saw me.

Now, perhaps you might argue that the reason they stopped gossiping when I came around was in fact that they'd been gossiping about me. I suppose that's possible. I don't know. I never asked them what they were gossiping about, and they never told me. But I never got any funny looks or heard any snickering, so I don't believe they were spreading any rumors about me. (After all, I really didn't give them much to gossip about.) Also, I maintained friendly relationships with all these fellow employees, and they felt comfortable enough to pass the time of day with me, have friendly conversations with me, and even confide in me about their personal problems, so I don't believe they gossiped about me.

I've also seen several negative outcomes when it comes to employees in the workplace who gossip. Rarely have I ever seen these situations end well. You may think that when you're gossiping, what you're doing is harmless—but trust me, it's not. And the person who ends up being hurt or damaged the most by your gossip is often yourself. I've seen otherwise hardworking, competent and qualified employees ruined by gossip and even fired, usually because of a toxic work environment that they themselves created with their own gossip. Even if their gossip didn't necessarily create a hostile work environment, it still didn't endear them to their bosses and higher-ups, especially since their superiors saw them spending time gossiping instead of working. And in some cases, the fact that they gossiped caused the person in charge not to trust them, and their advancement at the company (if they were fortunate enough to keep their job) immediately stalled.

So, don't do it. Just trust me on this. If you want to stay safe in your place of work, avoid gossip at all costs.

Listen to all sides of the argument before deciding or venturing an opinion.

Here's another way in which you can stay safe in the workplace: Always give room to both sides of the argument.

For example, you should refrain from expressing an opinion on a particular matter, at least until you've had the opportunity to listen to all sides involved. This will cause you to be unbiased in front of *all* your coworkers, which will in turn increase your popularity as well as your degree of safety at work. The people with whom you work will appreciate you simply for not getting involved, and they'll further appreciate you for offering a thoroughly considered and unbiased decision or opinion.

Let's consider this hypothetical situation (although, if I'm being honest, this has happened to me on more than one occasion). Two of your colleagues disagree on a particular matter related to work (and you're close and friendly with both colleagues). Both will of course attempt to win you over to their side. By not expressing an opinion or deciding until you've given both sides a chance to air their grievances, you enforce the notion of fairness (and that you're a fair employee who's not easily swayed by pathos). Knowing that you're not easily persuaded, they'll work even harder to win you over by presenting the best argument possible. And when you finally voice an opinion (after you've thoroughly considered every point of view), you'll be seen as the wisest, most clear-headed and unbiased coworker, and your opinion will be more highly valued than those of everyone else.

Let's take this illustration a step further. Two of your coworkers disagree with one another on a work matter, but you're quite close to one and barely know the other at all (perhaps because they're new or a transfer from another department). Even if you're inclined to favor the opinion or arguments of the person with whom you're closer, you should strive to reserve judgement and withhold your opinion or decision until both sides have been heard and considered thoroughly. If you remain unbiased, you'll be appreciated and considered a fair, unbiased judge, especially if your closeness with one of the coworkers is well-known. Over time, you'll probably become the one employee whom all of your coworkers may confide in at their time of need or argue their case to, simply because they know even friendships and interpersonal relationships don't impact your judgement, opinion, or decision-making rationale. Your fellow employees will work that much harder to win you over to their side, and you'll gain so much respect that whatever decision you make or opinion you express will become lauded as the wisest choice, even by those who were on the other side.

That, my friend, is respect you can't buy. It must be earned. How do you earn such respect and create such a degree of safety, popularity, and respectability for yourself? You simply remain unbiased and refrain from speaking your opinion until you've heard all sides of the argument.

Take your time before you give an answer or make a decision.

Take a good amount of time before you give anyone an answer. Who says you have to hurry? Some of the worst decisions I've ever seen in the business world were made on a whim, without being given proper thought or factoring in all variables.

So, take the adequate time to analyze all relevant factors, and make that important decision when you're *fully* informed. Save yourself the heartache, struggle, and possible flirtation with financial ruin and career derailment by taking an appropriate length of time to carefully consider each decision from every angle.

Let's go on with the previous example. Say that you've already earned the respect of your colleagues and garnered a reputation as a completely unbiased employee whose opinion is valuable. Well, how exactly do you maintain such a reputation? By not making a bad decision! Even if you become known as a totally unbiased coworker who gives equal weight and consideration to all sides of the issue, your opinions and decisions will quickly lose their value if they turn out to be horrible. Your coworker won't come to you for validation, no matter how unbiased they think you are, if your decisions turn out to be poor ones that lose the company money and/or cause trouble for everyone involved.

And, when it comes to decisions, I'm sure you've heard the proverb: Once bitten, twice shy. Opinions and decisions, especially when it comes to your place of work and the money that's coming in for the company, aren't light matters. If your coworker who comes to you for advice ends up getting burned by your poor choices, they're unlikely to ask for your opinion a second time and will defer to you only when absolutely necessary. This will radically decrease or even eliminate your degree of safety in your workplace and render you vastly unpopular—especially if other people's time, energy, effort, or money have been wasted or lost as a result of your poor decision-making.

So, it's important not only that you become known among your coworkers and superiors for making unbiased decisions, but also that you become known for making good decisions. And the only way to minimize your probability of making a poor decision is to thoroughly consider all facets of the decision.

This, of course, takes time. So, if you want to stay safe in the workplace, take an adequate amount of time to consider every angle before venturing an opinion or reaching a decision.

Attempting to maintain safety through the appearance of being busy is a temporary solution; inevitably, the truth will surface, and consequences will follow.

Who says you need to keep it up forever? Do you plan to retire from your current job? I'm not telling you not to work at all. Rather, you should make it *seem* like you're working and have plenty to do, even in the times when you're not so busy.

Remember that old saying, 'You're too smart for your own good'. If you finish your work too fast, not only will your work be more prone to errors, but your employer will also begin to expect that same tremendous, unsustainable, stress-inducing, burnout-causing level of speedy output from you whenever they assign you a project or give you a task to complete or a target to meet.

Advancement within the company is contingent upon demonstrating wholehearted dedication and effort.

Who says you shouldn't put your back into your work? *Of course* you should put your back into it! But at the same time, keep in mind the following: If you continuously surpass the targets, goals, and benchmarks assigned to you by large margins, your boss and/or bosses will inevitably raise the stakes. What if, two years from now, the targets they expect you to reach with ease become totally unreasonable and unattainable? This erodes your safety in the workplace and may even cause you to lose your position or your employers to lose their faith in you.

Thus, to stay safe in the workplace while continuing to add value to your organization and advance accordingly, you should attempt to meet or exceed your boss's expectations and the targets assigned to you, but not by too much. Just go a tiny bit above their expectations. And don't finish the work too fast, or else they'll expect that same tremendous and unsustainable level of output from you every single time without fail. Don't do that to yourself. Apply a reasonable amount of effort to your work and meet or exceed your employer's expectations, but don't go overboard. If you exceed expectations, exceed them by a few metaphorical inches, not by a mile.

In due course, individuals inevitably align themselves with a particular stance in a business. It's not feasible to consistently remain neutral or on the sidelines.

You may receive invitations or solicitations to join one group or another, but finding the middle ground and resisting the urge to join one group or the other will enable you to gain the respect of both groups. And if not, there's always Netflix ... and ice cream. Okay, I'm just kidding. But strive to be transparent and upright, no matter what sorts of challenges or arguments you're facing. Everybody will appreciate you all the more for it.

BEING SAFE—THE BOTTOM LINE

When it comes to being safe in order to create a stable work environment—one in which you escape office politics and any disputes between your coworker, and in which you keep reasonable expectations for yourself and have a set of goals and achievements that are feasible and attainable—there are a number of key points you'll need to implement to achieve a high degree of safety.

Firstly, stay safe at your workplace by avoiding conflict through remaining neutral.

By being team Switzerland, avoid getting needlessly involved in office conflicts or wars. There are many things you can do to keep yourself out of such situations. And if you find yourself pulled into the conflict, do your very best not to choose any side, but instead remain as neutral as humanly possible.

By remaining unbiased when it comes to office conflicts, and avoiding gossip at all costs, your coworker will develop a high degree of faith in your decision-making capabilities and in your ability to hand down impartial judgments and opinions. A high level of respect for you that will be engendered in your coworkers by your balanced, impartial opinions and decision-making. It will also ensure safety and stability, both among your peers and those in a higher position in your workplace.

Secondly, stay safe at your place of business by looking busy during work hours.

Stay safe by looking busy. Look busy while continuing to do whatever you need or want to do, since the average employee actually works only three (or fewer) hours out of eight hours each day. By projecting the image that you're busy doing things and working on the tasks assigned to you, not only will your bosses and your peers get a good impression of you as someone who works hard, but you'll also avoid being needlessly saddled with excessive workloads and your coworkers' unfinished work. You'll also avoid the situation where your boss sets ever-higher (and eventually unattainable) goals and targets for you because you've been continually exceeding their expectations by a significant (and ultimately unsustainable) margin.

Thirdly, stay safe at your place of business by being empathetic toward your coworker and peers.

Showing empathy to your fellow coworker will boost the confidence your peers have in you and make you more popular among them. Being empathetic by providing a willing ear for their concerns and personal issues will engender a high level of trust between you and your coworkers, who'll be more willing to treat you as their confidant. This level of friendship, relatedness, mutuality, and trust in the workplace will make your level of safety ironclad. If you build up these relationships, your fellow employees will also be more willing to defend you and speak up on your behalf when they perceive you're being wronged.

By adeptly avoiding conflicts and maintaining a neutral stance, one can create a safe and harmonious professional environment. Cultivating empathy for colleagues further contributes to a positive atmosphere. Additionally, the strategic approach of appearing busy not only enhances productivity, but also serves as a shield against unnecessary workplace tensions.

As you continue your professional journey, remember that mastering these skills won't only safeguard your wellbeing, but also pave the way for success. Embrace the insight shared in this chapter, and let it guide you toward a career marked by tranquility and achievement. Act today to implement these insights and shape a workplace experience that aligns with your goals and aspirations.

As we transition from the strategies of maintaining workplace safety discussed in Chapter 5, it's crucial to delve into a contrasting perspective in Chapter 6. Here, we explore additional aspects of playing it safe, focusing on the controversial tactics of blaming others, resorting to deception, and engaging in attacks on colleagues. Brace yourself for a deeper understanding of the intricate dynamics involved in safeguarding one's position at work, as we navigate the nuanced terrain of professional relationships.

CHAPTER 6
HOW TO BLAME OTHERS AND BE SAFE

Everything we hear is an opinion, not a fact. Everything we see is perspective, not the truth.

— MARCUS AURELIUS

In this chapter, I'll be talking about how playing the 'blame game' can actually get you closer to achieving your goals. While it may seem rather disturbing to many readers, the unfortunate fact of the matter is that this phenomenon—the blame game—takes place extremely often.

We may repeat to ourselves or others any number of motivational quotes and tidy inspirational speeches when people wonder exactly how we got ahead in our careers. These stories and quotes are fine and dandy, but the harsh reality of today's business world is that we too play the blame game far more often than we're willing to admit to ourselves, and we've more than likely advanced in our careers because of it.

WHAT EXACTLY *IS* THE BLAME GAME, ANYWAY?

Playing the 'blame game' is the practice of placing the blame on other people when things go wrong. To blame is to feel or declare that something or someone is responsible for a wrong or fault. And to blame others, or to play the blame game, is to redirect the responsibility for an error or wrongdoing away from yourself and at another person or group of people.

A key component of playing the blame game is that the person who plays the game evades taking any of the blame or responsibility themselves, even though a part of (or all of) the blame may actually lie with that person.

Blaming others for your own mistakes, wrongdoings, errors, or failures is a particular kind of defense mechanism. Playing the blame game might also be called a number of other names, including projection, displacement, or denial. Placing the blame on other people helps you to preserve your level of self-esteem, because you'll avoid awareness of any failings or flaws you may possess.

And being safe, as was covered in the previous chapter, refers to the practice of creating a safe and stable work environment for yourself.

Staying safe in the context of this chapter can be accomplished by playing the blame game, as we'll see in more detail below. In fact, playing the blame game is one of the easiest ways to increase your level of safety and stability at your place of business.

So, the significance of blaming others and being safe involves pointing the finger at others to maintain and increase your degree of safety at work. After all, since playing the blame game is a defense mechanism, it makes sense that the result of defending yourself using such a mechanism would be an increase in your degree of safety, doesn't it? Let's now consider this strategy in greater detail.

WHY DO PEOPLE BLAME OTHERS AND TRY TO BE SAFE? WHAT ARE SOME OF THE BENEFITS OF THIS?

It's much easier to blame others than to own up to our mistakes.

We blame others because it's so much easier than the alternative. Playing the blame game is a fairly effective defense mechanism, one that enables us to preserve our self-esteem while hiding our flaws. It's much simpler to play the blame game by finding a scapegoat for the problem, rather than owning up to the fact that the problem was of our own making. The sad reality is that most of the time, playing the blame game works. It's certainly far easier to blame others for something that's gone wrong than it is to take responsibility for the mistake.

After all, if you take responsibility for the thing that went wrong in your place of work, your bosses may not appreciate the fact that you're morally upstanding. Instead, they may begin to subconsciously (or consciously) assign blame to you whenever something goes wrong. This may cause them to perceive you as less capable, which may prevent you from advancing within the company.

When seen in this light, owning up to your own mistakes and failures (instead of playing the blame game and blaming others) seems to have little upside, other than the fact that you can consider yourself a morally upright employee.

In the best-case scenario, your boss and your fellow employees would *also* be morally upright people with a great deal of discernment. If this were the case, they wouldn't fall for any blame game tricks, and would respect you more because of your moral rectitude. But unfortunately, the sad truth is that many of us have bosses, managers, and colleagues who aren't so morally upstanding, and who may not appreciate any of your attempts to take responsibility for the mistakes being made and avoid playing the blame game. This is why the blame game is played so commonly in organizations all over the world.

Blaming others is a great tool that can be used to attack them.

Playing the blame game can be an excellent tool for attacking others. When it comes to those colleagues who antagonize you, playing the blame game provides the perfect opportunity for you to get back at them. As the old saying goes: Don't get mad, get even. So, if you want to get back at a person in your organization, retaliate against someone, or exact payback or retribution for someone wronging you, playing the blame game is an easy and effective way to do so.

Blaming others makes us feel safe and protects our self-esteem.

Playing the blame game makes us feel safe and serves to protect our self-esteem. This may be our own way of dealing with the 'unfair' outside world. In this case, the major problem is that we made the critical error of assuming that the outside world was fair to begin with. Thus, when we realize that the outside world is, in fact, not at all fair, we try to 'level the playing field'. We blame others unfairly because we may feel that we ourselves are being blamed unfairly or would be blamed unfairly. Thus, playing the blame game can enable us to feel protected in this otherwise utterly unfair world.

As mentioned, the blame game also preserves our self-esteem by shifting the blame away from ourselves. For instance, if something goes wrong, and is at least partially our doing, we may rationalize the situation by deflecting. For example, we might say, '*It was actually Bobby's fault that things went wrong*'. By blaming Bobby, we shift the blame away from ourselves and save ourselves from having to admit that we had something to do with that failure. Because if we admit to ourselves that the failure had something to do with us (or was entirely our fault), self-esteem-lowering thoughts may enter our heads, such as notions that we're good for nothing, stupid, or worthless. This can damage our self-esteem, hindering our ability to work effectively in the future. Whenever we encounter a similar matter, we may second-guess ourselves and believe that we can't do a good job and will fail again (because we've already failed once before). Playing the blame game avoids all of that and keeps our self-esteem (and potentially our future work performance) at a high level.

Blaming others helps us to stay safe in our workplace.

Playing the blame game by blaming others at work, especially for our own shortcomings, mistakes, and failures, can end up gradually making our position within the company safer by degrees. This may be a rather petty and contemptible thing to do, but more often than not, it works. This is because whether or not we realize it, we actually live in a culture of blame. Whenever someone besides us gets the blame for something that goes wrong, we're flooded with a great sense of relief. This happens far more often than we're willing to admit. We may not enjoy seeing ourselves in this light, but if we're honest with ourselves, we'll realize that we really don't like getting blamed for anything (even if it *is* our fault).

Further, playing the blame game allows us to stay safe in our place of work. This is because if the blame rarely (or never) falls on us, it's likely that our bosses will never think we're at fault. If we play the blame game successfully for long enough (and our bosses aren't discerning enough to see through our strategy), then when something goes wrong, we'll almost never get the blame for it. The person we're most successful in blaming will instead, because they've already been blamed so many times. Our bosses will automatically assume that it's that person's fault when something goes wrong.

This sort of subconscious blame assignment occurs even in the best of bosses (including the ones who always try to be fair). It's simply human nature. To keep this behavior from occurring, a boss must be extremely discerning and actively guard against automatically assuming that someone is to blame. But this requires a lot of discernment, and most bosses are too busy dealing with other things to spend so much effort on being fair (even if they want to be).

Thus, after a person plays the blame game successfully at their workplace for long enough, their level of safety in that workplace will be substantially elevated, because they'll rarely get the blame whenever anything goes wrong (even if it's their fault). This will preserve their position and safety in the workplace by protecting them from being fired. They'll also be more likely to be promoted or considered for advancement, since they never get the blame for anything and are thus perceived to be mistake-proof.

Blaming others is due to the fact that people inherently lie.

People are inherent liars. As Dr. House likes to remind everyone frequently, 'Everybody lies'. This is one of those things that's sad but true. We may lie for a number of different reasons, but we all lie. Lying is a characteristic inherent to the human race, when someone (especially a person in a position of power over us) asks us about what went wrong or whose fault it was that something went wrong. If the fault lies with us, our natural instinct is to lie. We blame someone else to protect ourselves from receiving the blame and the negative perceptions that come with it.

If we've been trained (or have trained ourselves) to become more morally upright, we may have overcome that automatic instinct to play the blame game in order to protect ourselves. But a significant number of people haven't trained themselves in such a way and either succumb to their automatic instinct of blaming others (these people may feel guilty about this later) or actively blame others without even thinking or feeling guilty about it.

AN ALTERNATIVE POINT OF VIEW

*The search for a scapegoat is
the easiest of all hunting expeditions.*

— DWIGHT D EISENHOWER

HOW DO PEOPLE BLAME OTHERS AND STAY SAFE? WHAT ARE SOME EXAMPLES OR ANECDOTES WHEN IT COMES TO PLAYING THE BLAME GAME?

By exposing the shortcomings of others (often in comparison to our own strong points).

Some employees show the shortcomings of others in opposition to their own achievements. By contrast, their achievements seem even more impressive, while the shortcomings of the people they blame seem greater. I've seen this happen more often than I'd like to admit.

I knew of one such employee who worked for a shoe company. He was excellent at many of the strategies listed in this chapter (as well as some of the strategies outlined in the following chapter). Let's call him Mike.

Mike was excellent at selling shoes. He could sell himself (and, by extension, the shoe) to pretty much any customer who walked through the door. But Mike was incurably lazy, and it affected the morale of the rest of the store. Whenever he was working, he was only ever concerned about the commission he'd earn from selling shoes to the customers. He never cared about keeping the store clean, restocking the shoes, moving the shoes from the warehouse to the sales floor, and so on. In other words, even though he didn't do the vast majority of tasks assigned to him, he considered himself the greatest employee because he was so good at selling himself to the customers.

Whenever he was assigned to work, he'd always man the cash register, even if specifically forbidden by the store manager to do so. This is because the manager knew that whenever Mike worked at the cash register, he'd do literally nothing else in the whole store, leaving it messy and displeasing to the customers who walked in. Not only would he do nothing, but he'd also order his fellow employees around, telling them to do the work that had actually been assigned to him.

Once, in an ultimately futile attempt to encourage him to be a more responsible and productive employee, the store manager told him that he was the future of that franchise. The words went to his head and served only to increase his level of bravado around the store, although he still did basically nothing except stand at the cash register and count out the commission from the transactions he'd made.

So how exactly did Mike play the blame game? The other employees of the store usually made fewer sales than Mike (because they were always much busier doing necessary things like cleaning the store, restocking the shelves with shoes, and organizing shoes). After all, if no-one ever restocked the shelves, or unloaded the shoes, soon there would be no shoes in the store for Mike or anyone else to sell. That is why working the cash register was supposed to be the last priority for Mike and he was supposed to finish all his own work first. But he'd instead order the other employees to do his work for him. Sometimes they did it, sometimes they didn't. Once, an employee politely refused to do his work for him because she already had a great deal of her own work to do. He then ran to the person in charge of the store that day, accusing her of being belligerent and making trouble.

From that day forth, every single conversation Mike had with this employee was utterly inflammatory. He'd say things to insult her specifically, and when she'd speak a word of retort, he'd run to the store manager and accuse her of starting an argument. He also got his only two friends at the store to treat this employee harshly. Further, knowing that his own sales at the store were superior to everyone else's, he'd always emphasize their relatively lower sales in comparison to his own. Also, when the person in charge of the store told this employee to tell Mike to do this or that task (which he had been assigned to do from the very start of his shift), he'd run to one of his friends and tell them that the employee who'd told him what to do considered herself better than he was. In this way, he poisoned some of the other employees against this one employee. He made this employee so miserable with his poisonous (yet admittedly skillful) playing of the blame game that she eventually wanted to quit working at the shoe company, despite the fact that she was one of the most conscientious and faithful workers at the store.

Eventually, Mike was told by the owner of the store that if he caused any more trouble with any of the employees, he'd be fired.

(At first, the owner considered transferring him to another store, but Mike pleaded his case and managed to stay.) However, even though he'd been warned, he continued to provoke his coworker. He'd do so in a way that was slightly more subtle, and when he was done provoking her, he'd run to one of his two supporters in the store and say, 'It's just useless to try to have even a pleasant conversation with her'. (Note that Mike had only said provocative things to her, and when she refused to respond or raise her voice at him, he then ran to his supporters to poison their minds against this employee.) Eventually, the employee he kept on provoking decided to quit working at the store, and he kept working there. But the point is that he made the other employee so miserable with the blame game that, even though he did basically no work at all in the store and she was a faithful and hardworking employee, she received no protection and became miserable enough to quit working at the store. By contrast, he didn't receive much of a punishment.

By playing the blame game to make others miserable and achieve their own ends.

A great friend of mine left his position at a top IT business, because although he was (and is) an exceptional code writer, his team manager didn't like him. So, his manager played the blame game with the company bosses and got under their skin, making my friend's life miserable until he left. Afterwards, the big bosses realized their mistake, his team manager got fired, and they tried to bring my friend back, but to no avail.

This is an extension of the strategy that Mike employed. Anyone that my friend's manager considered outwardly (or even silently) critical of him was made miserable by the blame game, which he played to the point where they wanted to (or even decided to) quit.

By using others to play the blame game for them.

You can play the blame game by working through proxies such as your peers and colleagues who can carry your message further. This is called manipulation, and you may be considered an expert at manipulation if you're able to get others to do your bidding without them realizing it. Once again, it doesn't sound pretty, but it happens, whether we admit it or not.

In the following chapters, we'll delve more deeply into the practice of manipulation by examining an example of a master manipulator. Here, the point is that you can get other people to play the blame game for you by sowing seeds of discord and playing your coworkers against one another.

It's important to emphasize that engaging in the blame game goes against both ethical principles and moral values.

This is certainly true, but, as Tyr Anasazi from the *Andromeda* series states: 'In my experience devils very rarely wear horns and carry pitchforks'. Those who are immoral and unethical enough to play the blame game to get where they want to go are much more common than you realize. You may encounter some of them at work (or you may even be such a person yourself).

Discussing accountability in the workplace is crucial, as it directly impacts professional relationships and could have serious consequences, including the risk of termination.

Playing the blame game can get you fired only if you get caught. In my business experience, both in the private sector and in the government sector, I've seen people gain a great measure of success by applying this method. More often than not, those who use this method succeed in achieving their ends, whether it be, for example, a promotion, advancement at the company, or a raise.

Engaging in the blame game skews our perception of who we truly are.

This may be true, but since you're already playing the blame game anyway, you probably won't see the difference, no matter what those around you may say. In your mind, they'll always be wrong, and you'll always be right. Wrong, but right.

BLAMING OTHERS AND BEING SAFE—THE BOTTOM LINE

The simple fact of the matter is that everybody lies. Everybody. Some lie sooner or later, due to a variety of reasons. And some of us may lie less than others while some of us lie all the time, even without feeling guilty about it. And some of us practice the blame game often in order to cover up our own lies or our own shortcomings and protect our self-image, our perception of ourselves, and that of the world around us. It may not be pretty, but then again, the truth is seldom pretty.

You can improve and even become an expert at playing the blame game.

You can actually become better and better at playing the game. You learn, you improve, you evolve, and you adapt. Some of us are able to become masters at this game and can even build a career around it. There are several different strategies for playing the blame game, and some people can find the perfect strategy that works for them.

Playing the blame game is the easy way out.

It's definitely easier to play the blame game than it is to be held accountable for your own shortcomings. It may not be *moral*, but it's certainly easier. And playing the blame game can serve your short- and medium-term goals. You can use the successful playing of the blame game to promote your own ends, to get rid of coworkers whom you dislike or who argue with you, to make yourself safe in your workplace, and more.

So, make sure you protect yourself from being blamed. Now that you're aware of it, be aware of who's doing it, along with how and why they're doing it—all while avoiding the blind spots.

CHAPTER 7

HOW TO CLAIM CREDIT FOR YOUR COLLEAGUES' WORK

*If you complain, it's not going to work out in
your favor 95 percent of the time.*

—FORD R MYERS (2019),
THE WALL STREET JOURNAL

In this chapter, I'll be speaking about how some of our colleagues move forward in their careers by essentially stealing ideas from others—whether they're peers or the people who are working within their teams. This phenomenon occurs far more often than we realize or would care to admit. Often, a colleague won't speak up for themselves and will stand idly by and watch their credit be taken, thereby enabling this phenomenon to occur more often than it should.

*It is amazing what you can accomplish
if you do not care who gets the credit.*

— HARRY S TRUMAN

WHAT DOES IT MEAN TO CLAIM CREDIT FOR THE WORK OF YOUR COLLEAGUES?

The practice of claiming credit for the work of one's colleagues is based on the fact that a number of people in any organization will do a certain amount of work, whether it's individual or team-based. A person who does a certain amount of work expects to receive credit for it. Credit, in the context of this and the following chapter, is defined as the public acknowledgment or praise given or received when a person's responsibility for, or role in, an action or idea is made apparent to others. Credit can also be defined as the ascribing of an achievement or a positive quality to a person.

At work, receiving credit for work done usually results in your boss, manager, superiors, and/or coworker looking more favorably upon you. Gaining credit in your workplace is thus vital to your advancement within the company, as well as obtaining the goodwill of your peers and superiors.

To claim or take credit for your colleague's work is to steal their idea, contribution, or work by saying that it was you who came up with that idea, made that contribution, or did that work. The practice of taking the credit for someone else's work can be likened to stealing someone else's completed test paper, erasing their name at the top, and filling in your own. This is an attempt to get the teacher or the professor to assign the grade of that person to you, so that you take that person's credit.

Applied within the context of this chapter, stealing the work of your colleagues constitutes an attempt to elevate yourself in the view of your superiors and fellow employees, enabling you to gain goodwill and favor in the eyes of others like your bosses without having to do much (or any) of the work.

WHY DO PEOPLE CLAIM CREDIT FOR THE WORK OF THEIR COLLEAGUES? WHAT ARE THE BENEFITS?

Once you successfully claim the credit for your colleagues' work, they won't often fight back.

In most cases, what's done is done. This means that if you've already managed to claim the success of one of your fellow employees as your own, that employee usually won't fight back, simply because they may lack the leverage required to resist your tactics.

Always seeking to claim the credit for your colleagues' work causes you to be proactive.

Seeking to claim the credits of your colleagues' work makes you more proactive as an individual. You'll always be on the prowl, looking for an opportunity to strike. This may not be the most orthodox way to do things, but is actually one of the most efficient ways to succeed in this dog-eat-dog world of ours.

We may not want to admit that this is the world we live in, but we face this harsh reality one day or another. In such a case, you'll realize that the most successful people are the ones who are always looking for opportunities to strike. These people are always on the alert, ready for any chance to steal the work or credit of a fellow coworker. They find such opportunities because they're actively looking for them. We may not *like* this fact, but these people's proactive mindset helps them advance in the business world.

You can claim credit that doesn't belong to you by overemphasizing your own contribution.

Gaining more credit than your colleagues is possible simply by overemphasizing your own contribution. The phrase 'It's almost always about the packaging' means that you must know how to oversell your accomplishments. This may not be an ideal solution, but it's technically less damaging than digging a proverbial pit for your colleagues by outright stealing their work. Instead of stealing credit for work you didn't do, simply do *some* work ... then overstate its importance. Using this strategy instead of stealing the work or credit outright can make you feel better about yourself at the end of the day, since you're not causing significant harm to your fellow coworker. As it's also much more subtle, your coworker may not realize you're doing this. At the same time, it elevates your standing in the eyes of your boss and helps you advance at work. This is a more subtle and slightly less harmful way to claim credit that makes you feel like you didn't really take advantage of others.

Of course, you're indeed taking advantage of them, since they're not getting their fair share of credit. However, the subtlety of this strategy makes you and everyone else believe that you're not digging a pit beneath them. Executing this strategy properly is often a tricky business, because you have to learn to overstate your accomplishments and oversell what you did to your boss and your coworker without appearing to brag. If you come across as boastful, your coworker may take offence and tell your boss that what you did wasn't actually significant. This strategy can usually be pulled off only with practice, because you have to learn to overemphasize your achievements in a matter-of-fact tone that doesn't draw your coworker's notice (but still impresses your boss).

Stealing credit for colleagues' work gives you more influence within your workplace.

Claiming credit for colleagues' work offers you the spotlight. If you're prepared to sell yourself in this way, one or two successful credit-claiming events can provide you with tremendous influence within your company, all but ensuring your long-term success. If you successfully claim the credit of your fellow employees' work and/or overemphasize your own contributions to a project a few times, your boss and the other higher-ups in your company will associate you with those achievements. This mere association in their brains can often be all you need to climb the corporate ladder.

Someone higher up may, for instance, remember the work you did on a particular project (because you oversold your work or stole someone else's). Consequently, they may decide to give you more responsibility, a chance to work on a more difficult project, a raise, and/or a higher position in the company. So, successfully claiming credit for your colleagues' work of overstating your own accomplishments can have a huge payoff in terms of risk versus reward (or effort versus results).

Claiming credit for colleagues' work can make you seem like a leader.

In business, perception is almost everything—bosses seldom care about petty fights in the office among underlings. So, if your bosses end up perceiving you as the proverbial leader (one who doesn't get caught up in petty squabbling), they'll likely assign further projects to you. Afterwards, you'll need to deliver, of course, but that's beyond the scope of this chapter.

Even if your fellow employees try to resist your stealing of their contributions and credit by accusing you, it may backfire, because the boss may see them as petty troublemakers who are always looking to pick a fight with their coworker. Those who are considered troublemakers are unlikely to advance very far in their organizations. The boss may in fact consider them not worth the trouble, and simply fire or demote them.

Often, bosses don't actually care who's right and who's wrong. The fact that the fight began in the first place is what bothers them, so they may tend to get rid of the people who start fights. This keeps the person who's stealing the credit in a safe position. It also makes them seem like a leader, because they're 'rising above' the fray and not responding to accusations or fights. The one who's pointing the finger at someone else usually tends to look the worst, even if the person they're accusing is guilty.

Strangely, we tend to sympathize with the *accused* rather than with the accuser (similar to our tendency to root for the underdog). Those who claim credit for their colleagues' work take full advantage of this odd quirk of human nature, making themselves seem like workplace leaders who are above petty squabbles.

AN ALTERNATIVE POINT OF VIEW

Appear weak when you are strong, and strong when you are weak.

— SUN TZU

HOW DO PEOPLE CLAIM CREDIT FOR THE WORK OF THEIR COLLEAGUES? WHAT ARE SOME EXAMPLES?

By befriending others and manipulating them to do the work

There are numerous ways in which you can take credit for work that's not your own. Some of us may be master manipulators. We befriend coworkers simply to gain access to their work or take advantage of them by getting them to do the heavy lifting. Indeed, some of us are 'leeches'. We can choose to ignore it—but we all know that whether or not we like this, it definitely happens (far more often than it should).

The thing about master manipulators is that as a victim, you often don't even *realize* you're being manipulated. I encountered one such master manipulator several years ago. A friend of mine (let's call him Mark) was his target. The master manipulator (let's call him Pete) worked for the same company as my friend in the same division. Pete saw that Mark was a hard worker, but noticed that he was also somewhat gullible and a tad lonely at his workplace. (One of his only friends at the company had just been transferred to another state to oversee a new branch.) Pete saw in Mark the perfect target for manipulation, and he struck with a vengeance.

Of course, it didn't seem to Mark as if Pete was manipulating him. That's because Pete started off slowly. He began sitting with Mark for lunch day after day. He didn't impose himself or force Mark to eat with him, of course. Instead, he asked politely one day if he could sit next to Mark and eat with him. Mark, being a kind and trusting person, said yes. Eating lunch together every day became their regular habit. They began to converse with each other throughout the day, and not just small talk by the water cooler. Whenever Pete found a subject of interest (whether work-related to or not), he didn't hesitate to head over to Mark's desk and chat with him about it. Pete and Mark also began to hang out together after work. Mark genuinely believed that Pete was doing all of this in the name of friendship. He never suspected any sort of ulterior motive.

Master manipulators are usually able to bide their time, because they possess an almost endless supply of patience. Pete and Mark had been close for several months before Pete began to execute the second part of his strategy. (Mark didn't realize this at the time. It was only *after* he'd been manipulated by Pete for quite a while that he finally understood what had happened and when it had started.) After being friends for months, Pete called Mark one day and asked him to cover for him with the boss. You see, Pete was going to be over an hour late (due to a traffic accident, or so he said). Pete had never been late to work before, so Mark was more than willing to explain this to the boss for him, and the boss was quite understanding. But here, Pete was only testing the waters. He was making sure Mark would support him in these sorts of situations, so began with a small thing like being late to work. When he determined that Mark was more than happy to cover for him, he saw the opportunity to take further advantage. Pete, the master manipulator, started off slowly but gradually sped up.

The next thing Pete asked Mark to do was to cover for him when he missed a project deadline. It was Pete's mistake, though it was probably done intentionally to determine if Mark would cover for him. Pete confessed his error to Mark, who felt terribly sorry for him and offered to take the blame. Pete at first refused (another master manipulator move) but eventually agreed, after Mark assured Pete that the boss liked Mark and would forgive an offence like missing a deadline once in a while. So, Mark willingly took the blame for Pete's mistake—his missed deadline. And the boss did indeed forgive Mark, since this sort of mistake or failure was rather out of character for him.

So it started out with relatively innocuous things: a missed deadline here, a small cover-up there. Mark was always happy to cover for Pete, because he considered him a good friend (his best friend at the company) and thought that Pete had his best interests at heart and wasn't intentionally making these kinds of mistakes.

Then, Pete began to escalate things. One day, he called Mark and asked him if he could help with the project that had been assigned to him, because he was going to be busy that day. The excuse he gave to my friend was that his mother wasn't feeling well and he needed to take care of her at her house. Mark gladly acquiesced to his request, even though he had work of his own to finish. Mark ended up staying up all night to finish his own project as well as Pete's. Ultimately, he did the entire project for Pete, but he did so with a willing heart, thinking he was doing it for a good cause (because Pete needed to take care of his mom). Once this happened, Pete knew his manipulation had been successful.

These occurrences of Pete asking Mark to do his work for him began to happen more and more frequently. He wouldn't usually ask Mark to do the whole project for him—but more often than not, when he asked, Mark would finish twenty-five to seventy-five percent of the work for him. Sometimes, he would start a project for Pete (or do fifty to ninety percent of it) and Pete would pick up where Mark left off and finish up the project, calling it his own. And Pete always had a good excuse, a good reason why he was unable to do the project that day. After a while, Pete had literally turned Mark into his unwitting slave. Pete even confided in Mark one day that he'd just been diagnosed with a serious disease (a confidence which turned out to be completely false), and Mark felt so bad for him that he did almost all of the work which was assigned to Pete for two entire weeks. Mark was happy to do the work for Pete, because he considered him a good friend and he trusted him.

This went on for nearly a year. Pete wouldn't always ask Mark to do his work—sometimes it was only once or twice a week, or once every two weeks. But the stress of doing one-and-a-half to two workloads began to take its toll on Mark, especially after the two-week period in which he thought Pete had just been diagnosed with a disease. He began to suffer from severe sleep deprivation and burnout, and the quality of his work began to dip. He still believed whatever Pete told him (in terms of Pete's excuses as to why he couldn't work).

The boss, noticing that Mark was constantly exhausted and that the quality of his work had decreased, asked him what was going on. Mark didn't want to get Pete in trouble (such is the brilliance of the master manipulator who befriends his targets), so he refused to tell his boss what was happening and why he was so tired all the time. But after the boss questioned him again (and even threatened to fire him if he didn't tell him why the quality of his work decreased), Mark finally admitted to the boss what was happening—the fact that he was being coerced into doing a large portion of Pete's work.

Mark and his boss began to compare notes. On one of the days during which Pete had asked my friend to do his work for him because he was supposedly taking care of his sick mother, the boss had seen him at a coffee shop, eating and laughing with a number of friends. Mark's boss also commented that he had no idea that Pete was suffering from a disease. He called Pete in to get to the bottom of the matter (and offer him extended sick leave if necessary). The boss was sympathetic to Pete, but such a matter required official documentation. Pete hastily produced a doctor's note, but the boss (who was already slightly suspicious due to his seeing Pete with his buddies) was able to determine that the note was a forgery.

Mark, whose faith in Pete had been shaken by his discovery that Pete's supposed illness was a complete fabrication, finally realized what Pete had been up to all this time. He called Pete to confront him, but Pete (knowing that the game was up) never answered his phone call. He avoided Mark completely from that point onward. Not only that, but Pete also quit his job immediately (before getting fired) and quickly moved away and got another better job without listing Mark's boss as a reference.

Pete was apparently charismatic and capable enough that his new employer hired him on the spot without calling his past employers to check, partly due to the impressive list of projects he had listed on his resume, many of which had actually been completed by Mark! Mark found out all of these details later on, but by that time, it was too late. Pete had moved on to a different company and a new set of targets.

Such is the power of the master manipulator. This is just one example, of course. Not every master manipulator will function in a similar fashion. But Pete saw in my friend a perfect target for manipulation and took advantage of him mercilessly. The entire process (from the moment Pete started befriending Mark until the day his manipulation and deceit was finally exposed) took more than a year and a half. Pete had Mark doing much of his work for him for almost an entire year; he listed all those projects and accomplishments on his resume, getting a new job on the strength of those accomplishments. So, Mark not only unknowingly did Pete's work for a year, but also contributed to his being hired somewhere else for more money.

As far as Mark can tell, none of the excuses Pete used to manipulate him into doing his work were true. Pete's mother lived halfway across the country, so there was no way Pete could've been going to her house to take care of her on those days. And he wasn't ill.

My friend was greatly saddened that he'd been manipulated and taken advantage of in such a way by a person he considered to be a good and decent friend. But that's the thing about master manipulators. Everything they do is calculated (down to the very first 'May I sit here and eat lunch with you?'), with an ulterior motive. Trusting people like Mark are all too easily taken advantage of by these master manipulators. They tend to prey on those who like to think the best of people.

Mark is one who always sees the good in people. He was certainly stung by this experience. I warned him to be wary from then on so that he'd no longer be taken advantage of in the same way.

My friend came out of this experience hurt but a great deal wiser. He won't be so easily taken advantage of next time. He still likes to think the best of people (and hopes never to run into or work with another person like Pete), but he's more reserved and careful nowadays.

Manipulating others without their knowledge

The more manipulative you are, the better. The true art of manipulation (paraphrasing Sun Tzu) is when you do it *without* the manipulated party even knowing it. This can clearly be seen in the example above. Mark had absolutely no idea he was being manipulated masterfully by Pete until he was confronted with the actual evidence of Pete's betrayal, manipulation, and deception.

Being informed about the thing for which you're claiming credit

Most people who choose to claim credit for their colleagues' work tend to know a great deal about the ideas or the projects they're stealing. It's in their nature to be informed, and they end up not only stealing the work but also making it their own. The best credit-stealers actually improve the work. The fact that they know so much about what was done makes it extremely difficult for their bosses to tell that they're not actually the ones who did the work.

Whether these people make others' work their own by adding key segments here and there or by improving it as a whole, the key to making it look like someone else's work is entirely theirs is to be thoroughly informed about it. This makes these people look great in front of their bosses at staff meetings or when asked for an overview of the work. They chime in immediately about all relevant points before any of their coworkers get a chance to say something. The fact that they say everything notable about the work makes it seem like their coworker didn't contribute anything significant to the project.

Pete employed this strategy to a limited degree as well, especially when he'd have Mark do the bulk of a project for him. On these occasions, Pete would swoop in and finish whatever small percentage was remaining and make it seem like he was improving the project as a whole. He even did this on some of the projects that had been originally assigned to Mark! He would say something along the lines of, 'Hey, do you need any pointers on that project of yours? Let me take a look at it'. Mark, ever so trusting, would always happily comply and be grateful for whatever tips, improvements, or pointers Pete would give him about his project. Pete usually wouldn't cut in to talk about all the relevant points of a project before Mark had a chance to speak, because that would've been too obvious. Unbeknownst to Mark (until after Pete had been exposed), Pete would sometimes go and talk to the boss about Mark's projects, making it seem like he himself had done significant work on them (but always emphasizing that Mark was still a hardworking and deserving employee). Pete made himself look good, taking the credit from Mark without doing much work at all—and without Mark realizing he was being taken advantage of until the very last hour.

It's unethical to steal or take credit for someone else's ideas.

This is no doubt true—but if others do it to you, should you turn the other cheek? Remember, this is business we're talking about, not church. So, an argument can certainly be made for fighting fire with fire instead of turning the other cheek. By claiming credit for someone else's work, you may feel like you're levelling the playing field or making things a little fairer for yourself in an otherwise unfair world.

While acknowledging your achievements, it's important to consider that some colleagues might raise objections regarding the attribution of credit for their contributions.

The key to handling the colleagues who speak up for themselves is to always appeal to their self-interest rather than their kindness (unless that's one of their defining qualities). If you steal credit from someone, make sure to let them know what's in it for them.

Attempting to take credit for your colleague's work of may lead to your marginalization within the company.

This will happen only if you don't play your cards right and implement these strategies properly and with great care. See the answers above.

CLAIMING THE CREDITS OF YOUR COLLEAGUES' WORK— THE BOTTOM LINE

Seeking to be proactive and beating others to the punch will yield several benefits.

Be proactive in your approach, as this can have numerous benefits for you. Beating others to the punch will elevate you in the eyes of your boss and will make it seem like you deserve the credit for your coworkers' work.

Make the most of every opportunity.

Seize opportunities when they occur. Remember that if you're waiting for the opportune moment, others who aren't looking for it may fail to make the most of their opportunities, thus creating an additional opportunity for you.

Work smart (not hard) by taking credit for other people's work.

As Estée Lauder once said, 'I never dreamed about success. I worked for it'. Work smart, not hard. In some cases, this may mean taking the credit from others. It's not as if taking the credit for other people's work is an easy task! You have to be proactive, always be ready to spot opportunities, and implement these strategies with care and precision. It can take a lot of patience and determination, as seen with Pete and Mark's example.

CHAPTER 8

HOW TO CLAIM CREDIT FOR EVERYONE'S WORK

Taking credit for other people's work doesn't make me selfish. I give plenty of blame when things fail.

— YOUNGHRMANAGER.COM

In this chapter, I'll be talking about how some people build entire careers by taking credit from their colleagues. This is what many books on businesses, working together, and so on, don't teach you. It's great to collaborate, but many of our colleagues simply don't care about the rules.

How exactly does this chapter differ from the previous one? Well, in addition to reiterating the principles which were previously discussed, it focuses on claiming the credit for the work or contributions of multiple people at once.

WHAT DOES IT MEAN TO CLAIM CREDIT FOR EVERYONE ELSE'S WORK?

As I said earlier, the practice of claiming credit for the work of others is based on the fact that the people in an organization will do a certain amount of work, and will expect to receive credit for that contribution. Credit can also be defined as the ascribing of an achievement, a contribution, or a positive quality to someone.

At work, receiving credit for work done usually results in your boss, manager, superiors, and/or coworker looking more favorably upon you. Gaining credit in your workplace is thus vital to your advancement within the company, as well as obtaining the goodwill of your peers and superiors.

For instance, your boss saying to you, 'Good job on that report you turned in yesterday' is an example of receiving credit for work done. The fact that your boss approves of the work done on the report may lead to your promotion or advancement. This is because your boss may see you as more capable and able to take on more responsibility due to the good work you've done.

To claim or take credit for your colleague's work is to steal their idea, contribution, or work by saying that it was you who came up with that idea, made that contribution, or did that work.

For instance, when using the example from the previous paragraph, the practice of taking the credit for someone else's work would involve the following: One of your coworkers writes the report. But before they get any credit for that report, you cause your boss to believe that it was *you* who authored it. Thus, you get the 'Good job on that report you turned in yesterday' from your boss instead of your coworker (the one who *actually* wrote the report and who *deserves* the 'Good job' from your boss).

For the more specific focus of this chapter, claiming the credit for everyone's work involves doing this on a larger scale (stealing credit for multiple reports from many different people or taking credit for the work of your whole team, for example).

As I said earlier:

… stealing the work of your colleagues constitutes an attempt to elevate yourself in the view of your superiors and fellow employees, enabling you to gain goodwill and favor in the eyes of others like your bosses without having to do much (or any) of the work.

When applied specifically to this chapter, stealing the work of multiple people at once involves dividing and conquering and is a speedy and fairly effortless way for a person to advance quickly within their organization, since that person is taking advantage of multiple people at once. This can enable a person to gain a lot of favor from their superiors very quickly.

WHY DO PEOPLE CLAIM CREDIT FOR THE WORK OF EVERYONE ELSE? WHAT ARE SOME OF ITS BENEFITS?

You show everyone that you're driven.

Claiming the credit for everyone's work shows everyone that you're driven and will stop at nothing to achieve your goals.

You achieve a measure of leadership.

As detailed in the previous chapter, claiming credit for the work of a colleague makes you an informal or proverbial leader, which can certainly create additional benefits for you within the company. Claiming credit for the work of multiple people at once can be an even more effective way of positioning you as a team leader of sorts.

Let's review why taking credit for other people's work can make you seem like a leader.

In business, the main issue is how you're perceived. Bosses don't usually care about petty fights in the office among underlings, such as the ones which may occur if you steal other people's work and they try to argue with you about it. You technically have no reason to argue with your coworker, since you're the one doing the stealing. (You don't have a problem with your coworker; it's your coworker who has a problem with you.)

Thus, if your superiors end up perceiving you as the proverbial leader (one who doesn't get caught up in petty squabbling), they may assign more projects to you and give you more responsibility and opportunity for advancement. Afterwards, you'll need to deliver on those projects and extra responsibilities, of course, but that's again beyond the scope of this chapter.

Even if your fellow employees try to resist your stealing of their contributions and credit by accusing you, it may backfire, because the boss may see them as petty troublemakers who are always looking to pick a fight with their coworker. Those who are considered troublemakers are unlikely to advance very far in their organizations. The boss may in fact consider them not worth the trouble, and simply fire or demote them.

The fact that bosses don't generally care who's right and who's wrong lends success to this credit-stealing strategy. The fact that the fight was started in the first place is what annoys them, so they may be more likely to get rid of the people who begin those fights and arguments in the workplace, considering them unprofessional. This keeps the person who's stealing the credit in a position that's altogether safe. It also makes them look more like a leader, because they're choosing to rise above the fray and aren't responding to or being provoked by the accusations.

As I said in Chapter 7, the one who is accusing and pointing the finger at someone else usually tends to look the worst, even if the person they're accusing is completely in the wrong:

Strangely, we tend to sympathize with the accused rather than with the accuser (similar to our tendency to root for the underdog). Those who claim credit for their colleagues' work take full advantage of this odd quirk of human nature, making themselves seem like workplace leaders who are above petty squabbles.

This strategy can be even more effective when applied in the context of stealing credit from multiple people. If several of your coworkers are angry at you for stealing their work and start to point fingers at you, you may look like a helpless, innocent victim who's being attacked by an angry mob. Your boss may end up thinking that all those coworkers have it in for you and sympathize with you even more. Since you're the only one who's not fighting (or even speaking up to defend yourself), your boss may defend you in their mind, and you'll be elevated in their esteem. You'll be the employee at whom everyone's taking shots—and even though the shots are well-deserved, your boss probably won't know that.

This will engender much more sympathy for you. To your boss, you may even seem like a 'Jesus' of sorts, taking all sorts of abuse from a mob of angry people without having earned any of it. It's likely, then, that your boss will reward you with a greater degree of leadership and more responsibility, thanks to the strong and upright character you've made them believe you possess. The fact that you're seemingly willing to take all sorts of abuse without breaking down or fighting back separates you from your coworker, causing you to transcend them, and makes you seem like leadership material in the eyes of your bosses. This is because leaders and other people in positions of responsibility often have to take a lot of flak for their decisions. Your boss may see you in this light and regard you as someone capable of handling such a leadership position and all the stress and negativity that comes with it.

You create more visibility for yourself within the organization.

Claiming the credit for everyone's work creates a much greater degree of visibility for yourself within the company, because no matter what others say, the first impression counts, particularly in the eyes of your managers and the company top brass. If you manage to constantly beat others to the punch, you'll be more visible. This is closely related to the phenomenon of how claiming credit for the work of your colleagues serves to give you the spotlight. Let's review that concept.

HOW TO CLAIM CREDIT FOR EVERYONE'S WORK

Claiming credit for everyone's work gives you the spotlight, which makes you more visible within the organization. But you must be prepared to sell yourself in this manner.

If you're prepared to sell yourself in this way, one or two successful credit-claiming events can provide you with tremendous influence within your company, all but ensuring your long-term success.

If you successfully claim credit for the work of your fellow employees and/or overemphasize your own contributions to a project a few times, your boss and the other higher-ups in your company will associate you with those projects or achievements.

This is what 'beating others to the punch' really means—that you're able to make yourself and your contributions more visible to your bosses and higher-ups than your coworkers are. The mere association in your bosses' brains of you with certain notable projects or accomplishments can often be all you need to climb the corporate ladder.

Someone higher up may, for instance, remember the work you did on a particular project (because you oversold your work or stole someone else's). Consequently, they may decide to give you more responsibility, a chance to work on a more difficult project, a raise, and/or a higher position in the company. So, successfully claiming credit for your colleagues' work of overstating your own accomplishments can have a huge payoff in terms of risk versus reward (or effort versus results).

This principle applies to an even greater degree when you're stealing the work of multiple people, simply because multiple people can do a lot more work and complete much bigger projects. If you can successfully make yourself the only name which the bosses associate with one of these huge projects (which may have involved twenty people or more), you're basically set for life. Why? Because these huge projects which require many people are often a defining moment for a company—some of the most prominent, time-consuming, successful, profitable, and memorable projects the company's ever produced. So, if you can oversell yourself, chime in early and beat others to the punch (before your coworker get a chance to say anything), be super-informed, and overshadow all your coworkers when it comes to this huge project, your name may be the *only* one the higher-ups associate with it. It's just human nature. The first impression is what matters, so if your bosses' first impression is that you're the main person associated with the project, that's what will stick.

You learn how to sell yourself.

Claiming credit for the work of everyone else teaches you to become better at selling yourself. If you plan on building a career using this strategy, you must always be adapting to your environment and ready to beat others to the punch. But here's the catch, and it's a big one: *You have to make it seem like this isn't the case* (particularly to those from whom you take the credit).

This principle relates closely to how the best manipulators manage to manipulate people without their knowledge. Just as Pete in the previous chapter took advantage of Mark without my friend having the faintest clue about the matter, those who claim the credit for the work of others do so most successfully when others can't tell what they're doing. Pete knew exactly how to sell himself to everyone (especially to my friend and his boss), and was thus able to pull the wool over their eyes for a pretty long period.

The long-term strategy Pete took in taking advantage of my friend probably wouldn't have worked if Pete were trying to take credit for the work of multiple coworkers. (After all, Pete invested a lot of time and energy into making my friend believe that he and my friend were pals.) But this doesn't mean that learning how to sell yourself and talk yourself up to others isn't an effective strategy when trying to claim credit for the work of multiple people. Quite the contrary, in fact. If you sell yourself effectively to all your coworkers, they'll collectively think of you as a friendly and agreeable person as well as a hard worker and someone whose approval they desire. Once this is accomplished, you can take advantage of multiple coworkers at once without them ever even realizing it.

You can gain more control.

Claiming the credit for the work of everyone else helps you to gain better control over your peers and your colleagues. By using the *divide et impera* ('divide and conquer') principle, you can sow the seeds of discord among your colleagues. This strategy must be executed with great caution, as it can backfire on you easily—but if it's executed perfectly, your coworker won't even know what hit them.

The key is for you to sow seeds of distrust that cause all your coworkers to suspect and not trust one another, *while still trusting you*. This is tricky, but if you do it successfully, you'll reap the ample (if immoral) rewards. All your coworkers will come to you to confide in you and complain about the other workers, and you'll be able to water those seeds of distrust and watch them grow. Then you can pick apart your coworkers with surgical precision and scoop up all the credit belonging to all of them, all the while seeming like a leader and a trustworthy person to your coworkers as well as your bosses.

As I said, it's an exceedingly difficult strategy to implement, but the rewards (though morally icky) are enormous.

AN ALTERNATIVE POINT OF VIEW

The 'divide and conquer' method is actually a more efficient technique than we may initially realize. How can you successfully claim the credit for everyone else's work? What are some examples?

Downplay taking credit for their work and learn to negotiate.

You can successfully claim credit for the work of everyone else by downplaying it. So, when an angry colleague comes to you and makes a scene, be sure to appeal to their interest rather than their emotional side. Respond to their anger in a soothing way. This will gradually bring their level of anger down. Then, make it seem like they have everything to gain *if and only if* they allow you to take credit for their work. You can try giving them incentives—like how they're taking one for the team this time, so you'll take one for the team next time, or how another coworker would appreciate and respect them more. Try appealing to their better nature or more generous instincts.

Above all, be sure to paint a picture for them of how good they'll look if they allow you to take credit for their work.

Every coworker will be mollified in a slightly different way, so practice and find out what works for each person. Perfect your negotiating skills and become an expert.

Learn how to get your colleagues to make fools of themselves.

You can successfully claim credit for everyone else's work of by getting your colleagues to make fools of themselves. You can achieve this if you trigger them and know what makes them tick.

For instance, if they make a scene and call you out during a meeting with your bosses, they'll make a considerable error and lose credibility. This can clearly be seen in Chapter 7: 'Claiming the credit for the work of your colleagues can make you seem like a leader'.

I've seen this happen all too often throughout my years in the business world. And when I've discussed the matter with friends and family, I've noticed how unaware most people are of the importance of perception in business. My friends and family usually tried to defend themselves when their work was being stolen—but this often ended with negative consequences for them, because they were seen as troublemakers. They were perceived as the unprofessional ones, when in fact it's the people who stole credit from them who should've been considered unprofessional. But they're so good at what they do that they make everyone else look like fools as they raise their voices and cause scenes, while the credit-stealers remain cool-headed and professional.

Control your tone when you're presenting.

You can successfully claim the credit for the work of everyone else by making sure you present everything as 'information', not as 'bragging'. So, your tone matters in addition to everything else. If you 'inform others' rather than 'brag', you stand to gain a lot more than you would in any other scenario.

This relates closely to the matters of selling yourself and of overstating your accomplishments or contributions to a project (see Chapter 7: 'You can claim credit that doesn't belong to you by overemphasizing your own contribution'). The key is your tone, which needs to be matter-of-fact and informational. Take any hint of swagger or bravado out of your voice. Your voice needs to convey information authoritatively, yet without any hint of boasting.

Taking credit for the work of others is both unethical and unfair.

This may be true, but it's unfortunately one of the facts of life. Frankly, life isn't fair either. Also, the colleagues or bosses who do this have their own motivations—motivations that may actually be ethical. It's quite a paradox.

Acknowledging the contributions of your team is crucial; attempting to take sole credit for their work may have negative consequences and impact your professional trajectory.

This depends on how you play your cards and implement the strategies from this chapter and the previous one . It also depends on how proactive you are, as well as how good you are at selling yourself and overselling your accomplishments.

While I may not be perfect, I strive to conduct myself in a manner that reflects my best qualities, and engaging in such actions isn't aligned with my principles.

Never say never, because some people may actually do this to secure their jobs or positions. One day, you may find yourself to be one of those people.

CLAIMING THE CREDIT FOR EVERYONE'S WORK— THE BOTTOM LINE

Someone will almost certainly try to take the credit for your work.

The world isn't fair. You just have to get used to the idea.

And for many, being an ethical individual sometimes includes presuming the same of others; nevertheless, be prepared for one particular moment of truth. Someone's inclination or attempt to take the credit for your work might come when you least expect it.

If someone tries to take credit for your work, take it as a learning experience.

As Nietzsche said, 'What doesn't kill you makes you stronger'. Learn about your colleagues and their character, as this lesson can actually be good for you in the long run. My friend from Chapter 7 was made stronger and smarter through his horrible experience with Pete. Seek to learn from any such negative experience.

If someone tries to take the credit for your work, proceed with the utmost caution.

Finally, choose your steps for resisting these credit thieves carefully. Calling them out immediately may backfire (see the above sections about how stealing credit makes a person seem like a leader), so if you do plan to fight back, choose carefully when to do it, if at all. Remember that you can always live to fight another day. Don't make rash decisions that you may later come to regret. Calm down, breathe, and analyze the situation thoroughly before making your move or your counterattack. Try not to descend into petty squabbles (or have your boss think that you're causing trouble and starting fights).

In summary, we've shed light on the unsettling practices of unethical employees who cunningly appropriate credit and ideas, exploiting the efforts of their colleagues and the collective work environment to their advantage. The stealthy nature of this intellectual property theft often goes unnoticed, highlighting the need for vigilance in professional circles.

As we transition into the next chapter, our exploration takes a broader turn, delving into the concept of sycophancy. Brace yourself for a comprehensive examination of the dynamics at play in a generalized sense, as we navigate the intricate terrain of workplace relationships and the pursuit of personal gain. The journey continues as we unravel the layers of workplace dynamics in our quest for understanding and improvement.

CHAPTER 9

HOW TO BE A SYCOPHANT

> *Beware of sycophants; they come in various ways and dimensions. They make you do a lot for them when they'll not as much as lift a finger to help you. They leave you drained with a little or no energy to help yourself and others that genuinely need your help. Know where to channel your energy.*
>
> — UNKNOWN

In this chapter, I'll be delving into what it means to be a sycophant and how I've seen such individuals manifest in the workplace, both in the private and the public sector. Whether we accept them or not, we must realize that sycophants are everywhere, and they manage to 'suck up' to their superiors in a wide variety of ways, from excessive flattery, to seeking opportunities, to confusing co-workers, to ... you name it.

WHAT DOES IT MEAN TO BE A SYCOPHANT?

According to the dictionary, a sycophant is a self-seeking, servile, insincere flatterer. It can also refer to someone who acts in an obsequious manner toward another person who's important in order to gain favor and advantage.

In the context of a workplace, a sycophant is generally an employee who sucks up to someone in a position of power. To 'suck up' is to be ingratiating or fawning. The term can also mean to gain the approval of someone in authority or a position of power by doing and saying friendly and helpful things which aren't sincere.

For instance, if a boss has five employees working for them and one of those employees is a sycophant, that employee would probably say various flattering things to the boss every day, complimenting them on their appearance, manner of speaking, charisma, and management style, for example. Further, that employee would probably offer the boss coffee and/or pastry of their choice. The sycophant would frequently tell the boss how powerful, awesome and/or wonderful they are in order to curry favor with them. Also, the work that the boss does, the criticism the boss gives, and the ideas that the boss has would all be complimented excessively by the sycophantic employee. The boss thereby receives a continual stream of praise from that employee.

Sycophancy doesn't work on all bosses, especially when used to an extreme degree. However, some bosses may be somewhat vain and/or a bit insecure and can't tell that the employee's a sycophant. Instead, these bosses draw their self-worth from the flattering words of the sycophant, finding those words to be a continual source of support, encouragement and comfort.

You may read this chapter and realize that you have a coworker (or perhaps more than one) who's a sycophant, one who's always seeking to ingratiate themselves with the higher-ups. Or perhaps your inner eyes might be opened to realize that you yourself have shown some sycophantic behavior in the past. If you're the boss, or find yourself in a supervisory capacity, you may realize you have an employee who's trying to be sycophantic toward you. Or you may even be enlightened to the fact that you're vulnerable to this type of sycophantic behavior. Whatever the case may be, after reading this chapter, you'll be better equipped to recognize and deal with sycophantic behavior, whether you find it in yourself or in others.

WHY WOULD ANYONE WANT TO BE A SYCOPHANT? WHAT BENEFITS DOES THIS YIELD?

You can curry favor with those in positions of power.

Being a sycophant allows you to obtain favor in the eyes of your bosses. This is the major reason why sycophancy has been in practice since (and before) the time of Ancient Greece. Even if you exhibit sycophantic behavior only occasionally, your boss will most likely be flattered by that behavior and will look more kindly upon you as a result.

Many bosses aren't discerning enough to see when someone's being a sycophant towards them (especially if the behavior isn't laid on too thick). So even if your bosses despise sycophants, they may not even realize you're being a sycophant toward them, especially if you don't go overboard. Sometimes, a little goes a long way.

Other bosses (who may be insecure, vain, and/or have other issues) may actually *prefer* their employees to act sycophantically toward them. For these bosses, surrounding themselves with at least a few sycophants gives their self-esteem a boost, as they draw their valuation of themselves from the words of the sycophants who work for them. And since sycophants will never say anything negative to them and will only flatter them continually, their self-worth gets elevated and they believe they're doing an excellent job or having great ideas (when the exact opposite may be the case).

The most skillful sycophant will flatter this kind of boss for taking a course of action the sycophant knows to be disastrous. At the same time, the sycophant can ingratiate themselves with someone even higher up—the boss of their boss—while suggesting their immediate boss isn't up to the task at hand. This sycophant is then simultaneously doing three things.

Firstly, they're finding favor in the eyes of their boss, who's susceptible to flattery and draws their self-worth from it.

Secondly, the sycophant's finding favor in the eyes of their *boss's boss* (who may also be susceptible to flattery or who may not have enough interaction with the sycophant to see them for what they are).

Thirdly, the sycophant's secretly undermining their immediate boss in the eyes of their boss's boss. For this skillful sycophant, the ideal outcome of this situation is to not only curry favor and become beloved in the eyes of both higher-up individuals (the boss *and* the boss's boss), but also to get the boss fired and take their place without the boss ever knowing it was the sycophant's fault they got fired. The boss may even praise the sycophant to the higher-up boss without ever knowing that the sycophant's stabbing them in the back.

You can become an expert in the art of negotiation.

Being a sycophant will make you an expert in the art of negotiation. Learning to navigate the sometimes-rocky sea of interoffice politics will teach you superb negotiation skills. As you're busy being a sycophant, you'll be placed into situations with your boss, with the other higher-ups, and with your fellow employees during which you'll be forced to negotiate your way. You'll become supremely skilled at dodging bullets, so to speak. Your desire to fulfil the whims and desires of your boss (the one toward whom you're exhibiting sycophantic behavior) will drive you to negotiate with your fellow employees regarding just about everything. You'll become the boss's yes-man, and you'll have to learn how to ensure your fellow employees comply with that 'yes'.

You'll become a proactive individual.

Being a sycophant will make you more proactive, since it places your focus on spotting opportunities rather than doing actual work. Although one might argue that if you were doing actual work, that would make you proactive, let's be honest: If you're seeking to take the path of the sycophant, you probably weren't doing much work to begin with.

Thus, actively seeking opportunities to ingratiate yourself with your boss means you'll be much more active than you were before. You'll proactively seek opportunities which will benefit you and allow you to curry more favor with your boss and/or the higher-ups.

You may reduce the amount of work you have to do.

Being a sycophant can actually *reduce* your workload, since you'll be able to manipulate others and get them to do the work for you. If you become an expert manipulator, you'll be able to get your coworkers to do everything for you while allowing yourself the time and space to gain a broader view of everything around you. Your workload will be reduced, and you'll also be freed up to spot more opportunities for being a sycophant and manipulating your coworkers.

You place yourself in a position to collect information on others.

As a sycophant, you'll be in a position to gain information on everyone at the office. This is due to the fact that you'll be ingratiating yourself with the boss, so they'll likely give you greater access to information than you would've had as a mere employee who's not a sycophant.

In the world of business, you'll come to realize that the only thing that matters is information. Information truly is power.

AN ALTERNATIVE POINT OF VIEW

Sycophant—One who approaches Greatness on his belly so that he may not be commanded to turn and be kicked. He is sometimes an editor.

— AMBROSE BIERCE

HOW DO YOU BECOME A SYCOPHANT? WHAT ARE SOME ANECDOTES AND EXAMPLES OF THIS?

Compliment your boss excessively.

Over the years, I've seen so many team members over-compliment their bosses simply to hide their shortcomings as well as the fact that they don't do a thing. And far too many bosses fall for this trick, allowing this kind of behavior to continue. While other colleagues are busy doing their work, sycophants are busy sucking up and gaining favor with their bosses and higher-ups.

See the previous section in this chapter, 'Being a sycophant allows you to curry favor with those in positions of power', for a hypothetical illustration: For this skillful sycophant, the ideal is to become beloved in the eyes of the boss and the boss's boss, then get the boss fired and take their place without the boss ever knowing that it was the sycophant's fault.

Sadly, this has happened multiple times to people I've worked with. I'll illustrate the point with one of these real-world examples. The sycophant, let's call him Al, worked directly under his boss, let's call him Tim. And we'll call Tim's boss Bill.

Bill was pressing Tim for ideas on the development of a new project. The major caveat was that the idea had to be completely original (because Bill wanted to be able to launch a product that wouldn't have any competitors initially). Al had already begun his sycophantic behavior toward Tim long before, and Tim had fallen for it and begun to trust Al more than any of the other employees who worked under him.

Tim went to Al and told him about Bill's desire for a breakthrough product. They had a private brainstorming session in Tim's office (only Tim and Al, since Al was more trusted than the other employees due to his sycophancy and favor-currying). This brainstorming session continued through happy hour, during which Tim and Al got drinks. However, Al saw an opportunity and merely pretended to drink. They had been spit-balling a few ideas—although technically it was Tim who was actually coming up with all of these, while Al, master manipulator that he was, was actually just tricking Tim into thinking that Al was *also* coming up with new contributions.

Al was certainly being proactive, though. Tim had a few good ideas, two of which were completely original. But Al, seeing his chance, downplayed those ideas and made Tim forget about them fairly quickly (hence the strategic decision to hang out). Tim also had another good idea, but it wasn't an original product; a competitor was developing such a product at the exact same time.

Al happened to know about this new product being developed by their competitor. But he kept this information to himself and began to work his sycophantic magic, telling Tim 'That's the one!' and 'Wow, I wish I'd thought of that myself' and 'Man, you're a genius'—things of that nature.

Al knew that Bill's major requirement for this new product was that it must be completely original. So, Al purposely kept from Tim any hint of information regarding the competitor's product development, praising Tim's idea in such a way that Tim thought it would be idiotic to present anything else to Bill.

At the same time, the two brilliant ideas which Tim had had (and which Al had downplayed and later made him forget completely) were carefully stored away in Al's brain. He researched both ideas and discovered that both were, in fact, original ideas, without any competing products being developed by any other companies. He drew up two proposals based on those ideas. But he did so in secret, without ever letting Tim or any of his coworkers know what he was busy doing. All the while, he helped Tim with his plan for a product that Al knew would be ultimately doomed in the eyes of Bill.

When the day to present came, Al said that he got a flat tire on the highway and needed to get it fixed (he didn't have a flat tire). Tim went in to present without him, but made sure to mention to Bill what an invaluable contribution Al had made to the plan.

But Al was there, sitting in the parking lot, waiting to pounce. Because of the trust that Tim had in Al, he called him immediately after the meeting ended to tell him that Bill had loved the plan. Al said that he'd gotten a temporary fix for his tire, so he could meet Tim at a restaurant to celebrate. They agreed to meet soon after they hung up the phone. Al watched Tim drive out of the parking lot and in the direction of the restaurant (Al had suggested one that was nice and far away).

After Tim's car was safely out of view, Al made his move.

Al walked into Bill's office. Bill was elated to see him, since Tim had told Bill of Al's work on the plan. But Al told Bill that he had serious reservations about the plan Tim had just presented, because he'd found out about a competing product development plan from another company.

Bill was furious. His main requirement (which he'd made exceedingly clear to Tim) was that their new idea be completely original, free from any potential competition. Bill was about to pick up the phone and call Tim to yell at him, but Al swooped in before he could. Al mentioned that he'd been working on a few ideas of his own in case the one Tim wanted didn't pan out. He then presented those two proposals he'd drawn up (both of which were actually Tim's ideas).

Bill, not wanting to celebrate too hastily a second time, took about twenty minutes to do some research, call his contacts, and make sure their competitors weren't developing anything similar. They weren't. So, Al became the instant hero of the hour. Al had of course carefully worded his conversation with Bill and placed all the blame on Tim for choosing the failed idea and not checking about a competing product. At the same time, he intimated to Bill that he'd come up with both of the new ideas he presented completely on his own.

Bill, still furious with Tim that he'd not done his research properly, and thrilled with the fact that Al had apparently saved the day, offered Tim's job to Al on the spot.

Poor Tim was still sitting at the restaurant, wondering what had happened to Al and not realizing that Al had just stabbed him in the back. Tim waited at the restaurant for over an hour. (Al didn't answer any of his calls or texts in that time.)

Once Al had securely stolen Tim's job and responsibilities, he finally reminded Bill to call Tim into the office to tell him that he'd been terminated. Bill asked where Tim was, and Al told him that he was at a restaurant. Bill promptly delegated the task of firing Tim to Al, sending him to that restaurant to fire Tim.

Al had planned his moves carefully, and had requested a table in the middle of the restaurant, where Tim couldn't easily make a scene without being embarrassed. But Tim would make no such scene. Al told Tim that Bill had sent him to let him go, and he explained that Bill had discovered a competing product being developed by another company right after Tim had left. (Al made it seem like Bill had discovered the competing product on his own.)

Because Al was such a master manipulator and sycophant, the way he broke the news to Tim left Tim despondent, but without any feelings of blame toward Al. Tim simply assumed that only someone in Bill's position with his level of contacts at other companies could've found out about that competing product.

Amazingly, Tim and Al departed from that restaurant, the scene of Tim's firing, calmly and as friends (or at least Tim *thought* they were friends). Al was comforting him in the best sycophantic way he knew how. So, Al left that restaurant thinking that he had nobody to blame for his firing except himself. Al, pretending to be a friend, even offered to pack up Tim's desk for him so he wouldn't have to show his face in the office again. Tim, feeling miserable and like a complete and utter failure, agreed. He didn't want to face Bill due the shame of having failed him in his sole requirement.

Al manipulated his fellow coworker into shunning Tim completely, so that he didn't find out immediately that Al had stolen his job as well as his ideas. It actually took a few months before Tim began to piece together what had happened; when the announcement for one of the products came out, Tim realized that the idea sounded familiar. He had the feeling that he'd actually originated the idea, but his memory of that evening was a bit foggy, so he shrugged it off as a coincidence. But when the second product announcement came out not long after, Tim thought that it couldn't be a coincidence. He remembered having that idea.

After contacting Bill as well as the employees who used to work for him (and who now worked under Al), with a bit of cajoling and persuasion, he finally gleaned the fact that Al had taken his job and his ideas. He pled his case before Bill, but Bill didn't believe him at all. The negative impression Al had given Bill on the day of the presentation was strongly ingrained and remained.

Then Tim filed a lawsuit against the company, specifically naming Al as one who'd violated his intellectual property rights. But Al's lawyer took full advantage of the fact that Tim had been drinking on the night of the brainstorming session (drinks which Al had recommended, but he certainly didn't let that slip), and Tim lost the lawsuit.

Tim lost out on the rights to those two ideas and all the fruits they bore. And he lost his job to the conniving, sycophantic Al.

This may be one of the most severe cases of sycophancy I've encountered, but it's by no means a unique story. Sycophancy is everywhere, whether it's subtle or blatant. Learn to watch your back and look out for the signs.

By confusing your coworker and taking advantage of the fact that they're enabling you

Sycophants behave the way they do because other employees allow it in one way or another. Some sycophants become so good at what they do that they constantly raise smokescreens and confuse everybody. They gain free time simply because they suck up to the right people, and while others are busy doing the heavy lifting, they're busy gaining favors. Irony and sarcasm, the two main modes of combat used by sycophants at the office, usually don't change.

Al from the above example was a master of creating smokescreens and confusing just about everybody he communicated with. He wove his web of deception intricately and deliberately. Tim, the unwitting fly, not only didn't realize that he'd flown into Al's web, but didn't even realize he was being eaten alive. Tim enabled Al's sycophancy (as did basically everyone else). And Tim paid dearly for it.

By looking busy and making sure everybody sees how busy you are

Sycophants can make themselves look busy. They have an inherent talent for it, and they make sure that absolutely everybody else sees how busy they are, particularly their bosses. They care about looking busy more than they do about anything else. However, they're not busy doing actual work; they're in fact sucking up.

Sadly, due to the various smokescreens they've created to confuse everyone around them, looking busy works for sycophants (most of the time). It certainly worked for Al. And he definitely did a lot of sucking up to Tim before the events in the example took place (enough to cause Tim to consider Al his most trusted employee).

Being a sycophant is frequently regarded as unethical.

Obviously, this is true. It's indeed highly unethical to be a sycophant. But the thing is, if a person is a sycophant, they almost certainly don't care about the fact that being a sycophant is unethical. This is one of the main traits of a sycophant: They don't care about anyone else but themselves. The sycophant has their own agenda, and that's the only thing they care to pursue. To a sycophant, everybody else is just a means to an end. A sycophant would never have such an ethical dilemma.

When it comes to dealing with individuals who opt to be sycophants, my options are somewhat limited, aside from employing irony and sarcasm in my approach.

You may be as ironic and as sarcastic as you like. Unfortunately, sycophants tend to thrive on such things. In fact, these sycophants will likely drive you to continue being ironic and sarcastic, as it will boost their sycophantic behavior.

While maintaining loyalty to my business, I can exhibit sycophantic behavior, distinguishing myself from other sycophants who lack loyalty to their businesses.

Denial is quite normal. Very few people care to admit to themselves that they're sycophants or that they exhibit sycophantic behavior. But please at least make an effort to analyze your own behavior. Have you begun any rumors at the office at least once? If this is the case for you, you could be well on your way towards becoming a sycophant. And once you're a sycophant, you'll most likely lose your moral compass and the ability to see whether you're still loyal to your business.

BEING A SYCOPHANT— THE BOTTOM LINE

Those who practice sycophancy are all around us.

Sycophants are everywhere. But you can certainly train yourself to spot them and be wary of their behavior.

Learn the characteristics of a sycophant—and be warned of the downsides of having one around you.

Sycophants are excessively sweet, make a lot of comments, and talk a lot (much more than necessary). The drawback of being the recipient of this sycophantic behavior is that these sycophants often then spread malicious rumors about you or other colleagues.

A sycophant will easily change their loyalties.

Sycophants are characterized by their shifting loyalties. They'll hitch their wagon to a rising star in order to rise with it. When the star can rise no further, they'll have no qualms in abandoning that star for another one that appears more promising. They'll attempt to ingratiate themselves with whoever they believe can further their careers and help them on the path to advancement within the organization.

CHAPTER 10

HOW TO BE A SUPER-SYCOPHANT

*An intelligent person believes in rolling up
the sleeves and pulling up the socks whereas
a sycophant is always ready to go down on
knees and taking off the pant.*

— ANUJ SOMANY

In this chapter, I'll be building on the content of the previous one and diving even more deeply into the phenomenon of sycophancy. Considering how extensively you may encounter sycophantic behavior and how systemically ingrained it is, both in private and public organizations, sycophancy deserves a more in-depth discussion. I'll also consider sycophantic behavior that's so advanced and prevailing that it may be considered 'super-sycophancy'.

WHAT DOES IT MEAN TO BE A SUPER-SYCOPHANT?

First, let's review the definition of a sycophant as it was discussed in the previous chapter. According to the dictionary, a sycophant is a self-seeking, servile, insincere flatterer. It can also refer to someone who acts in an obsequious manner toward an important person to gain favor and advantage.

In Chapter 9, we discussed how sycophants suck up to people in positions of power in a workplace. In this chapter, we'll take it one step further by endeavoring to study the phenomenon of the super-sycophant.

A super-sycophant is an individual who takes sycophancy to its most extreme heights (or, rather, depths). A super-sycophant is so abhorrently and ingratiatingly submissive and obsequious that they've lost all sense of limits or boundaries. They're completely willing to do literally anything and everything they can to please their boss. A super-sycophant no longer has any sense of restraint and will do literally whatever it takes to ingratiate themselves with the boss.

This goes beyond a mere or occasional occurrence of flattery or a compliment of the boss's hair, outfit, or managerial style. I don't like to even put into words exactly what lengths a super-sycophant is willing to go to, but since this is a chapter that delves into a consideration of super-sycophancy, I'll do so.

Go ahead. Let your imagination run wild. What are some of the worst things an employee might try to do to suck up to or 'get in tight' with the bosses or the higher-ups? The behavior of super-sycophants runs the gamut. Some of this super-sycophantic behavior probably crossed your mind. But I'll spell it out for you. Some things that a super-sycophant might stoop to in order to ingratiate themselves with the boss include the following: blackmailing other employees to figure out the weaknesses of the boss (or for some other nefarious reason), bribery, securing sexual favors for the boss, and committing crimes on behalf of the boss. This is by no means a conclusive list. These are just a few of the most heinous acts a super-sycophant is willing to undertake in order to suck up to the boss and thereby elevate their own career.

WHY WOULD A PERSON BECOME A SUPER-SYCOPHANT? WHAT ARE SOME OF THE BENEFITS?

Being a super-sycophant may have a positive effect on your career growth.

Being a sycophant can actually have a positive effect on career growth. There are studies that confirm this. It's all a matter of not setting overly ambitious targets. Essentially, one can become a protégé and move up the ranks through their super-sycophancy, whether in a private or public organization.

You can become more able to promote yourself.

Sycophancy can boost an individual's self-promotional ability. While arguably despicable, sycophants do have qualities: One of these is that they know how to sell themselves, usually through manipulation.

One such example is through comparison. They boast about their own accomplishments (although those accomplishments usually don't amount to anything) while downplaying the accomplishments of others.

You can boost communication as well as reciprocity.

Sycophancy can boost communication, as sycophants focus on immediacy (the 'Yes boss, right away boss' attitude) and reciprocity. A primary strategy of a sycophant is to impress their boss right off the bat, so this sort of yes-man attitude brings with it an automatic promise of speedy communication and reciprocity.

Unfortunately, the downside is that the sycophant may not be giving you the full story and is probably selectively giving you information (or falsifying information entirely) to achieve their own ends.

You can pursue your own agenda.

Sycophancy allows you to pursue your own agenda. While you suck up as much as possible, you're able to gain time to pursue your own plans, either within the organization or around it.

This can clearly be seen in the example of Al and Tim from the last chapter. Al used Tim (and Bill) as well as the situation itself to pursue his own agenda, all while making Tim believe that he was one hundred percent on his side.

You may boost your stability and your safety at your workplace.

Sycophancy can boost work stability. Everyone's relatively safe under the boss, and this works well enough in quite a few public and private organizations as well.

For instance, consider police stations or the hotel industry. Both of these are workplaces in which sycophancy and the yes-man attitude can boost your level of safety and stability as an employee. Bosses in these situations tend not to like employees who talk back to them or who offer negative criticism of them. So, the behavior of the sycophant works well in these situations (and others with a strong hierarchical structure).

A SHOCKING FACT

Sycophants always pursue promotions within an organization; they constantly transform within an organization and climb up so they can influence the decision-making process. At the same time, they influence and disrupt Human Resources or recruitment and selection processes.

They're rather resistant to individual change. They're more likely to try and lead an influential change in the organization itself than try to change themselves. Some of them start sabotaging the organization if it doesn't change in the way they want.

HOW CAN A PERSON BE A SUPER-SYCOPHANT? WHAT ARE SOME ILLUSTRATIONS OF THIS?

By finding a boss who prefers working with sycophants

As strange as it may seem, some bosses do prefer sycophants, although few people will actually admit it. This is because such bosses aren't actual leaders. While leaders welcome different opinions and embrace diversity, bosses who aren't leaders actually *prefer* sycophants, as they seldom argue with them.

Tim from Chapter 9, 'How to be a sycophant', is a clear example. In this anecdote, Al was such a sycophant, such a master manipulator, that he may be considered a super-sycophant. He lived and breathed sycophancy. But (as far as I know) he didn't descend into performing criminal or other such unsavory acts (other than stealing Tim's two ideas during the brainstorming session, but that crime was never proven). But other super-sycophants will do literally *anything* to get ahead. For these people, the end absolutely justifies the means. They don't care who they step on when they're on their way up the ladder.

By finding an organization that prefers to employ sycophants

I've actually seen organizations entering difficult times (some went bankrupt, some were purchased by competitors) due to the fact that their leaders weren't able to get divergent opinions, as all those around them never disagreed with them.

By being ambitious and scheming to climb the ladder

Sycophants are ambitious, and they scheme and plan their rise to the top. Some of them actually become so good at what they do that it becomes quite difficult to counter their webs of lies.

SOME OBJECTIONS TO BEING A SUPER-SYCOPHANT, AND RESPONSES TO THOSE OBJECTIONS

Discussing the potential repercussions of excessive sycophancy, it's important to highlight its detrimental impact on the workplace, posing a significant threat to the overall survival of a business.

Whether or not a workplace gets destroyed by super-sycophancy depends on the nature of the business itself. A hotel, restaurant, or even public organization can actually be an environment in which super-sycophancy thrives.

In the grand scheme of things, excessive sycophancy doesn't contribute to your long-term success.

This isn't necessarily true. There are people who have actually made a career out of being a sycophant. They've become so good at what they do that they manage to weave a network of deception, similar to that of a spider.

In a company with a robust code of ethics, it's unlikely for a super-sycophant to maintain a long-term presence.

This may not actually be true. Such super-sycophantic individuals are quite devious, and they're well-versed in bootlicking or apple-polishing, so there are very few things they're not willing to do to achieve their own goals. They may lurk in the shadows of those stronger than they are for quite a while without ever revealing their true intentions.

BEING A SUPER-SYCOPHANT— THE BOTTOM LINE

Those who practice sycophancy are everywhere, and you may occasionally encounter a super-sycophant.

Sycophants exist at all levels within an organization and always pursue their own agendas. Super-sycophants are encountered more rarely, but their effects can be devastating.

Some bosses actually *prefer* to work with a sycophant, because they make them feel validated.

Some bosses derive their sense of self-worth and self-esteem from the words of the sycophants around them. This may be due to a sense of insecurity or for a number of other reasons.

A sycophant who takes the practice of sycophancy to an extreme and is willing to do just about anything is a super-sycophant.

There are individuals who are so submissive, so abhorrent, that they actually become super-sycophants, meaning they're completely willing to do anything they can to please their boss.

CHAPTER 11

HOW TO BETRAY NUMBER TWO AND WIN

You have enemies in your life? Good. That means you've stood up for something, sometime in your life.

— WINSTON CHURCHILL

In this chapter, I'll be sharing several experiences which I've either lived or which have been shared with me concerning how some decent vice-presidents were cast aside or betrayed by the employees below them, simply because they weren't willing or able to pay attention to and/or observe the disgruntled people who were working below them.

WHAT DOES IT MEAN TO BETRAY NUMBER TWO AND WIN?

First of all, what do you mean by Number Two? Number Two, in the context of this chapter, refers to the person in the company who's second in command. Traditionally, this person may have the title of vice-president of the company. However, due to the rather varied and frequently complicated structures of companies and corporations, it's entirely possible that the *real* Number Two in the company may be the right-hand man of the chief executive officer (CEO), such as the chief operating officer (COO) or the chief financial officer (CFO). Alternatively, if the CEO of a company is Number One, the right-hand man of that CEO (who could be the COO or the CFO) might be known as the president of the company (and not as the vice-president). So, the Number Two position could be called the vice-presidency or the presidency, depending on how the company has been structured. Or, if the owner and/

or the founder of the company is not merely a figurehead and actually holds the power within the company, then the Number Two in this company may actually be the company owner's right-hand man, who's often the CEO. Or, if a company has a number of different cofounders, the Number Two in that organization may be one of the cofounders, the one who has the second-greatest amount of power in the company.

Now, allow me to discuss what it means to betray Number Two *and win*. The winning component of this strategy involves the success with which one is able to betray Number Two. Success, in this case, doesn't merely refer to Number Two getting kicked out, disgraced, demoted, or some combination of the three due to the actions of the person who's betraying them. In the case of the strategy being detailed within this chapter, for the employee doing the betraying, to win or to succeed also means that the employee derives some benefit from the demise of the Number Two.

Another optional condition for success is that no-one in the company knows that such a betrayal took place. In other words, a completely successful implementation of the 'betray Number Two and win' strategy would involve an employee betraying Number Two and getting them demoted, fired, and/or disgraced in order to take their place without anyone in the company even knowing that the new Number Two was the one who betrayed the now fired, demoted, or disgraced Number Two.

Winning may not necessarily involve an immediate promotion for the employee who implements this strategy. If the Number Two has been blocking the rise of this employee, then merely getting rid of Number Two may be considered a win for the employee who betrays them.

Similarly, it's not necessary that every single person in the company be completely ignorant of the act of betrayal for the implementation of the strategy to be considered a win. It's only necessary for the higher-ups in charge of the employee's advancement to be ignorant of that employee's betrayal.

It's better, of course, if one can pull off the betrayal strategy without anyone at the company figuring it out (because the gossip or open hatred exhibited by one's coworker may eventually reach the ears of the higher-ups in charge of the traitor's advancement, promotion, and career growth). But if one can't manage to hide their traitorous ways from absolutely everyone at the company, it may still be considered a success—as long as the higher-ups aren't direct witnesses to the betrayal. Anyone else at the organization who gets wind of the betrayal might be persuaded to keep their mouth shut through bribery, flattery, or some other means (such as the various strategies which have been discussed in the preceding chapters).

So, to put it in more succinct terms, to betray Number Two and win means to get the person in the Number Two position in the company fired, demoted, and/or disgraced in a way that doesn't block or hinder the possibility of further advancement and promotion for the party committing the act of betrayal.

WHY DO PEOPLE BETRAY NUMBER TWO? WHAT ARE SOME OF THE BENEFITS OF BETRAYING NUMBER TWO AND WINNING?

You can learn to ignore others.

When you're betraying Number Two, you quickly learn to ignore others. Ignorance is bliss, particularly in a workplace full of people towards whom you feel antipathy or who antagonize you. Moreover, you learn to hear only what you want to hear, meaning that you'll be able to become more selective in everything your ears come across and filter out whatever doesn't please you.

You can become a master of deception.

In quite a number of instances, this can prove very useful. Today's business world, whether we like to admit it or not, has become a battleground, seemingly built for the survival of the fittest. Those who don't adapt will eventually be cast aside.

You can become more observant.

Betraying Number Two can actually make you more observant of things happening around you. As a betrayer, or someone who considers betraying at some point, you must always try to be as attentive as possible to things happening around you. You learn, you evolve, you become better at it. You'll eventually become so good that you won't even have to fight any battles.

You can learn to accept defeat.

Betraying Number Two teaches you to accept defeat. As a deceiver, you'll taste defeat every now and then. After all, it won't work every time. But there are gains for you, even when you lose. What doesn't kill you makes you stronger, right?

You can become a more meticulous person.

Planning a betrayal teaches you to be meticulous. Planning and a cunning nature become your attributes. It teaches you how to evaluate your options, to plan for scenarios, while others become pawns in your game. Al from Chapter 9 was thoroughly meticulous in his betrayal of Tim.

AN ALTERNATIVE POINT OF VIEW

After all, what is a lie? 'Tis but the truth in masquerade.

— LORD BYRON

HOW CAN YOU BETRAY NUMBER TWO AND WIN? WHAT ARE SOME EXAMPLES OF THIS?

By learning about the weaknesses of your boss and exploiting them

A friend of mine lost his vice-president (VP) seat at a well-known company because he wasn't paying attention to those below him. They learned of his weaknesses and exploited them to the max. He was too proud or too blindsided to see what was happening right under his nose. Before he knew it, the board asked him to resign.

Here's what happened. Obviously, my friend had considerable talent and was a hard worker. Otherwise, he wouldn't have gotten the VP seat in the first place. The company considered my friend invaluable, and they definitely showed it. However, the employees who worked under him (some of whom had started at the same time and level as he had) grew frustrated with his apparent lack of interest in them. It seemed like once he got the VP job, he acted as though he was on a different level from them. Which of course, he was. He was the second in command at the company. But he assumed that he would have the same cordial relationship with those employees that used to work shoulder-to-shoulder with him and who now worked under him.

That is where he was wrong. Terribly wrong.

You see, relationships between coworkers require work to maintain. He was no longer spending much time with those who had been his fellow employees, so he shouldn't have expected to maintain the same relationships with them. Further, the fact that he was now VP of the company altered the power dynamic significantly. It gave him immense power over them, and they began to resent him for it.

Jealousy may also have been a factor in igniting this resentment against my friend, since some of those who now worked under him had started at the same time as he had and at the same level.

Due to his incorrect assumption that his previously decent relationships with those who worked under him would be maintained while he was their VP, he didn't pay much attention to them at all. They began to feel used by him. (Whether that was a just feeling or not, I can't say.) But management typically asks employees to do many things, and they normally do them without too much complaint. And perhaps they were irked that he'd risen from among their ranks and was in a position of power to order them around.

Regardless of their motivations, they began to resent him considerably. Because they'd previously been on decent terms with him, they took advantage of this fact to discover his weaknesses. They found all of them (all the ones that mattered, anyway). And boy oh boy, did they exploit them. My friend didn't know what hit him. He was like a deer caught in the headlights when all his faults and weaknesses were exposed. These faults became a public embarrassment for the company, so the board asked my friend, with all his skills and talents, to resign.

Ultimately, my friend's assumption that those who worked under him would respect him and continue to respect him was a costly one. Instead of respecting him, they resented and were jealous of him. This fomented a revolution, so to speak. Eventually, the board appointed one of his former fellow coworkers (one of the ones who had started at the same time and level as my friend) to take the vacant VP seat.

That is what you call betraying Number Two and winning.

By belittling Number Two in the eyes of Number One

Make it so that the Number One in the company doesn't notice the effort his Number Two puts in. This isn't always possible—but if it works, it works, and it may propel you forward faster than you can imagine. At the same time, however, remember that others may pursue the same route. So, if you do decide to go down this road, you're always risking that sooner or later, things may go south.

This case of betraying Number Two by belittling them in the eyes of Number One is exactly what Al did to Tim (the Number Two) in the eyes of Bill (the Number One), from the anecdote in Chapter 9. Al quite effectively betrayed Number Two by belittling (or downright sabotaging) the efforts of Number Two in the eyes of Number One. And in this case, it paid off handsomely for Al. After all, he got the job of Number Two and retained the relatively good opinion of everyone else. Even Number Two didn't have a negative impression of him for a few months. The sad thing is, Al is such a master manipulator that he's managed to stay in that slot to the present day (to the best of my knowledge).

Who knows? Al may be currently plotting a takeover of Number One and trying to figure out how to betray him. You'll read more on that in the next chapter.

By sabotaging the organization internally

Internal sabotage can push Number Two out. Take the example of professional football: If the players on a particular football team want to get rid of their coach, they simply need to play poorly for a few games. The coach is the one who pays the ultimate price of getting the sack, since the response of the team's owner and general manager is to fire the coach (or all the coaching staff) when the team isn't winning games, then try to rebuild from the ground up, not realizing that the players actually had the ability to win games previously. The games were merely lost due to the sabotage of the players.

But (one might argue) at least in the case of professional football, if the players don't like their coach, the coach won't get the respect and cooperation he needs from the players, and the players won't play with the same level of heart. So, the best thing for the organization may indeed be to fire a coach whom the players don't like. If the coach is causing problems or is generally disliked, the entire team will have a morale issue, which will affect gameplay. Hundreds of millions of dollars will very quickly go down the drain in such a case.

So, there's something to be said for betraying Number Two when the majority of the members of an organization agree that it needs to be done.

SOME OBJECTIONS TO BETRAYING NUMBER TWO AND WINNING, AND RESPONSES TO THOSE OBJECTIONS

Engaging in betrayal against Number Two while striving for victory isn't in line with ethical principles.

Betraying Number Two and winning is indeed a highly unethical act. But, sadly, I must confess that I've seen this practice manifest itself in every single business with which I've been involved, regardless of whether it was in the public or private sector.

Winning after betraying Number Two might have consequences that come back to haunt you.

This won't happen to you if everybody comes to understand that they mustn't cross you in any way. You don't have to convey this in a threatening way, but rather in a 'Let's keep to ourselves' kind of way. Others may actually come to see you as an informal leader.

Over time, trust has the potential to be restored.

This depends on the principles of each individual. For me, trust, once lost, can never be recovered. But then again, that may not be the same for others.

BETRAYING NUMBER TWO AND WINNING—THE BOTTOM LINE

Learning to betray Number Two and win will help you prepare to better defend yourself when someone tries to do that to you.

If you do decide to pursue such a path of betraying Number Two and winning, you should be better prepared to see the warning signs if someone tries to do the same thing against you.

Learning to betray Number Two and win will help you become more observant and attentive.

Such a path of betraying Number Two and winning is indeed dark, but it does help you become more attentive and observant to the world around you, especially when it comes to interoffice politics.

Here's a little titbit to rationalize away any of the moral qualms you might be having about betraying Number Two and winning.

'After all, what is a lie? 'Tis but the truth in masquerade.' This quote by Lord Byron basically sums it up and may help you rationalize your behavior if you choose to implement this strategy of betraying Number Two and winning.

Moving from the betrayal tactics against Number Two, the next chapter unveils the strategies employed to betray the ultimate authority, Number One. Get ready for a deep dive into cunning maneuvers and calculated risks as we explore how individuals manage to emerge victorious even when dealing with the highest echelons of power within the organization.

CHAPTER 12

HOW TO BETRAY NUMBER ONE AND WIN

Better an honest enemy than a false friend.

— GERMAN PROVERB

It can come as a shock if you find out a colleague took credit for your work, seemingly set you up to take a fall, or reportedly badmouthed you behind your back. The way you survive this type of situation should be based on the relationship and history you have with the colleague.

In this chapter, I'll be delving more deeply into the meaning and significance of betrayal as it relates to the office, how one can use office betrayal as a tool, and how one can benefit from the practice of office betrayal.

WHAT DOES IT MEAN TO BETRAY NUMBER ONE AND WIN? LET'S DISCUSS.

First of all, what do I mean by Number One? Number One, in the context of this chapter, refers to the person in the company who's in command, the 'Top Dog' or 'Head Honcho'. Traditionally, this person may have the title of president or chief executive officer (CEO) of the company, the chair of the board of directors, or even the owner and/or founder of the company. Often, if the owner and/or the founder isn't merely a figurehead and actually holds power within the company, they may also be the CEO.

So, the person who's Number One at a particular company may hold several titles within it. For instance, it's possible for the Number One at a particular company to be the founder, the owner, the chair of the board of directors, and the CEO all at the same time. Or, if a company has a number of different cofounders, the Number One may be one of them. It all depends.

Basically, the Number One is the person who has the ultimate say regarding all the decisions and who has the greatest amount of power. For instance, the Number One at Facebook would undoubtedly be Mark Zuckerberg. The Number One at Apple (when Steve Jobs was alive) was Steve Jobs. Now, the Number One at Apple is Tim Cook.

Now, allow me to discuss what it means to betray Number One *and win*. The winning component of this strategy involves the success with which you're able to betray Number One. Success, in this case, doesn't merely refer to Number One getting kicked out, disgraced, demoted, or some combination of the three due to the actions of the person who's betraying them. In the case of the strategy detailed within this chapter, for the employee doing the betraying to win or succeed also means that the employee derives some benefit from the demise of the Number One.

Another optional condition for success is that no-one in the company knows that such a betrayal took place. In other words, a completely successful implementation of the 'betray Number One and win' strategy would involve an employee betraying Number One and getting them demoted, fired, and/or disgraced in order to take their place without anyone in the company even *knowing* that the new Number One was the one who betrayed the now fired, demoted or disgraced Number One.

Winning may not necessarily involve an immediate promotion for the employee who implements this strategy. If the Number One has been blocking the rise of this employee, then merely getting rid of them may be considered a win for the employee who betrays them.

Similarly, it's not absolutely necessary that every single person in the company be completely ignorant of the act of betrayal for the implementation of the strategy to be considered a win. It's only necessary for those in charge of the employee's advancement to be ignorant of that employee's betrayal.

It's better, of course, if one can pull off the betrayal strategy without anyone at the company figuring it out (because the gossip or open hatred exhibited by one's coworker may eventually reach the ears of the higher-ups who are in charge of the traitor's advancement). But if one can't not manage to hide their traitorous ways from everyone at the company, it may still be considered a success—as long as those in charge of the employee's advancement aren't direct witnesses to the betrayal. Anyone else at the organization who gets wind of the betrayal might be persuaded to keep their mouth shut through bribery, flattery, or some other means (such as the various strategies which have been discussed in the preceding chapters).

In more succinct terms, to betray Number One and win means to get the person in the Number One position in the company fired, demoted, and/or disgraced in a way that doesn't hinder the possibility of further advancement and promotion within the company for the party who's committing the act of betrayal. An optimal outcome for the practice of betraying Number One and winning is to successfully take over their position as a direct result of that betrayal.

A sub-definition of betraying Number One and winning is the practice of destroying those who may be your competition (or otherwise in your way) when it comes to vying for the top job.

WHY SHOULD YOU LEARN HOW TO BETRAY NUMBER ONE AND WIN? WHAT ARE SOME OF THE BENEFITS OF BETRAYING NUMBER ONE AND WINNING?

You'll better see and grasp opportunities.

Learning how to betray Number One and win enables you to see the opportunities better. You'll become an expert at assessing situations.

For example, in many businesses, leaders will remain essentially unchallenged as long as the business is doing well and surpassing its targets. However, once the business slips up or misses one of its benchmarks (even if it seems to be something relatively minor), an employee who's looking for an opportunity to betray Number One and win can pounce at that moment. They can amplify that slip-up so that it becomes something bigger than it actually is, placing the blame squarely on the shoulders of the Number One, thus creating an opportunity for their own advancement.

You'll be forced to come up with sound arguments for the act of betrayal.

Learning how to betray Number One and win forces you to come up with arguments for the actual act of betrayal. You can never hope to win simply by arguing explicitly that you're better than Number One, so they should support you instead. That's not subtle, and almost never works in the real world. Instead, what you need to do is build your case using solid arguments (often through a lawyer), otherwise you run the risk of being cast aside as one who's trying to make a power grab.

Being prepared with definitive arguments will also serve to discourage any similar attempts others might make on you (once you become the primary leader), as such preparations will make you seem calculating.

You'll pay a greater degree of attention to informal communication.

Learning how to betray Number One and win causes you to pay more attention to informal communication within the business. Informal communication plays an important role in any business, and it's at least as important as formal communication, if not more so.

Recall the concept of 'corridors of power', made famous by C P Snow. The implication we can take from this is that the real power, the real decisions, and the most valuable information-sharing can often take place in the corridors during those informal moments of communication.

You'll be prepared for the fights which will come later on.

Learning how to betray Number One and win prepares you for the battles ahead. It's quite competitive out there, as I'm sure you know—so as you learn and prepare, you'll evolve your strategies and perfect your approaches.

You'll obtain greater vision.

Learning how to betray Number One and win grants you vision. Eventually, always being prepared and attentive to what's happening around you grants you a greater level of vision and allows you to sniff out any of your colleagues who may be seeking what you seek for themselves. Essentially, it's like a game of chess—you can end up knowing the moves your opponent will make even before they do. Thus, you can win any fight without having to do any actual fighting. This is the greatest form of victory, according to Sun Tzu.

AN ALTERNATIVE POINT OF VIEW

When we confide in a coworker and they break that confidence, or if harsh words are spoken, we tend to replay these events in our minds. It's human nature. The challenge becomes remaining professional so we don't fuel the fire or end up further entrenched in drama. Responding and reacting are two very different actions, so think long term.

— SHANDRA CARLSON

HOW CAN YOU PERFECT THE PRACTICE OF BETRAYING NUMBER ONE AND WINNING? WHAT ARE SOME SUCCESSFUL REAL-WORLD EXAMPLES?

By taking advantage of the rumor mill at work

Prior to a job interview for the position of the CEO of a certain company, one of the candidates started some nasty rumors about the other two candidates (indirectly, of course). Whether the rumors were true became irrelevant. The rumors caught on and spread throughout the company, making the two candidates look bad, and the candidate who started those false rumors got the job, simply because people were suspicious of the other two candidates, despite the fact that the rumors lacked any actual evidence or substantive backing.

By keeping yourself out of the groups in your workplace and avoiding socializing as much as possible

It's almost always better to stay out of any small groups at work. Some people don't socialize at all; they're happier and more relaxed in this condition. In the shadows, under the radar, they secretly plan to overthrow their bosses.

By being prepared with sound and rigorous arguments against any of the ideas which are being supported by your boss

Prepare rigorous arguments to combat any presentation your boss may decide to support in front of the board of the company (for example). But by rigorous, I do mean *rigorous*. You can't simply do nothing and expect to betray Number One successfully. This will take a great deal of planning, consideration and work.

SOME OBJECTIONS TO BETRAYING NUMBER ONE AND WINNING AND RESPONSES TO THOSE OBJECTIONS

Betraying Number One to achieve victory is both immoral and unethical.

Business leaders in today's world often have to make such decisions. It's a hierarchy, so sometimes the only way to climb the corporate ladder and achieve the ultimate level of success is to betray Number One and win.

Betraying Number One and achieving victory won't lead to a favorable future, as the reality of karma can't be ignored.

If you plan your moves with utmost care, you can even plan for whatever karma may bring. It depends on whether you leave any loose ends or not. Real leaders tend to leave zero loose ends, with no stone left unturned.

Despite my efforts, I won't be able to thwart the occurrence of such a successful betrayal against me.

You will be able to prevent this kind of betrayal from happening to you if you remain sharp and on the edge, as a real leader should be. And because you've already committed this sort of betrayal yourself, you should be ready for the warning signs when someone tries to attempt it on you.

BETRAYING NUMBER ONE AND WINNING—THE BOTTOM LINE

Don't try to betray Number One in a haphazard manner or when you aren't sure of the outcome.

I can't emphasize this enough: Never get into a fight with Number One when you aren't sure of the outcome. Instead, always thoroughly evaluate and assess the situation. You should 'strike' with your betrayal of the Number One only when you're all but certain of victory, or you risk losing much more than the battle itself. You risk the loss of your job—or even worse, your reputation.

Consider every possible outcome and tell as few people as possible of your plans.

You should always attempt to plan for unforeseen contingencies. Let as few people as possible know about your plans, or else you run the risk of facing a *Game of Thrones*–style ending within your company. Trust me, it's nothing good. Plan for those contingencies.

As we transition from the intricate strategies revealed in this chapter, where the immoral employees manage to betray even the highest authority within the organization and emerge victorious, the next chapter takes us deeper into their elusive tactics. This chapter unveils a fascinating yet concerning revelation: These individuals not only avoid detection, but thrive by seamlessly transitioning to a new job at a different organization.

The exploration of their success in securing new opportunities sheds light on their relentless pursuit, revealing that their ability to find more vulnerable targets is a key factor in perpetuating their deceptive practices. Join us as we delve into the cunning maneuvers that allow them to stay one step ahead and continue their questionable journey.

CHAPTER 13

HOW TO FIND A BETTER JOB BEFORE THEY DISCOVER YOU'VE BEEN DOING NOTHING ALL THESE YEARS

People don't quit jobs. They quit bosses.

—MARCUS BUCKINGHAM

Seventy-five percent of workers who voluntarily left their jobs did so because of the bosses and not because of the position itself, according to a poll by *Gallup*.

On average, an individual changes their career five to seven times during their lifetime. According to *Careers Advice Online*, roughly thirty percent of the total workforce changes jobs every twelve months.

In this chapter, I'll be discussing how an individual can leave their job and find a new and better one before they're discovered or exposed as a fraud or an employee who does nothing.

WHAT'S THE MEANING OR SIGNIFICANCE OF FINDING A BETTER JOB BEFORE THEY DISCOVER THAT YOU'VE BEEN DOING NOTHING ALL THESE YEARS?

For the immoral employees I've been describing in this book, this is one of the ultimate measures of the success of their implementation of these strategies and tactics. If you manage to find a better job before you're exposed as an immoral employee who's been using the strategies in the above chapters as your means of getting ahead, this is one of the ultimate signs of your success. After all, if you move to a better job before your company discovers who you really are and what you've actually been up to, then the danger of being discovered has more or less passed: You've succeeded in elevating your position, and are now fully free to begin implementing the strategies all over again at your new job (if you'd like to do so).

So, what does it really mean to find a better job? What's defined as a better job in the context of this chapter? A better job may be a job that gives you a higher position in the company (with a better title than you had before). Or a better job may be a job that offers you more money, bonuses, and benefits than the one you had before. A better job may even (ideally) be a combination of both, in which your position in the new company is higher than the position you left, with a higher salary (preferably significantly higher) than the one you received in your former position.

A better job might also be defined using more intangible measures. For instance, a better job might be one in which your boss views you more favorably than your previous boss did, or a job in which your fellow employees and peers (or even the higher-ups) are more easily manipulated. Some might consider a better job one in which the strategies within this book can be more successfully applied (hopefully without being detected).

But the most concrete measures of a better job are what you would expect them to be: A higher salary, more perks and bonuses, and a higher position, rank, or title within the company.

Here's one thing of note regarding a better job: In the context of this chapter (and indeed the entire book), finding a better job is defined as finding a job with a different company.

In the context of this chapter, finding a better job within the same company will do you no good, because if you stay within the same company, you run the risk of eventually being discovered and exposed as a fraud, an immoral employee, and a person who does nothing. But if you move to a different company and find a better job there, that's considered a successful implementation of the strategy contained within this chapter.

Let's examine the significance of the second part of the strategy in this chapter. The goal is to find a better job *before they discover that you've been doing nothing all these years.* So, you see, flying under the radar and implementing the strategies contained within this book without being detected is a key factor. Secrecy is vital.

The ultimate goal, then, is to change to a better job at a different company without being exposed or discovered at your former company. Ideally, your bosses will send you off to the other company with their full-throated support and wholehearted blessing (or, in an even better scenario, they'll fight to keep you and offer you perks, salary raises, and promotions that you can leverage at your new job to make your position and salary even better than before).

You might be wondering why this chapter contains the ultimate goal and strategy for the immoral employees described in this book. What about the chapter preceding this one? If you're wondering about this, allow me to explain. Chapter 12 explores how you can betray Number One and win. Refer to the definition of betraying Number One and winning in Chapter 12, 'How to betray Number One and win': The ideal outcome is to get the person in the Number One position fired, demoted, and/or disgraced and then to successfully take over their position as a direct result of that betrayal. If you implement this strategy successfully, you could end up CEO of the company (or in the position of the person who has the most power). And many of you might be thinking that that's the goal.

The ultimate goal, one might think, is to become the CEO or Number One at a company. And for some, this is indeed the case. But you may be forgetting one of the central tenets of this entire book. You want to get to as high a position as you possibly can while doing as little work as you possibly can. Remember the concept of doing nothing? And the strategy of doing nothing and getting promoted?

In case you've forgotten, you can refresh your memory with the following definition of doing nothing from Chapter 3:

Doing nothing means that you're not working toward a tangible goal or the production of a service or a product that would be considered a useful contribution to the economy or the world at large. Winnie-the-Pooh, by contrast, isn't technically doing absolutely nothing all day. He's breathing, singing, rummaging, eating his own honey, moseying about, visiting friends, conversing with those friends, stealing and eating the honey of those friends, and searching for more honey. But what Winnie-the-Pooh does is *considered* to be nothing due to the fact that his activities don't make a useful contribution to society; that is, his activities don't *add value*.

Doing nothing can also include procrastinating. As many of us may know, when we're procrastinating, we're often extremely productive at accomplishing a lot of things—everything except that which we're supposed to be doing. For instance, if you're working from home and you have a project which needs to be finished within two days, you may find that during that time, doing just about anything else—cleaning the house, running errands, fixing the grill, vacuuming, cleaning the swimming pool, helping your kids with their math homework, getting the leaves and mud out of the gutter, etc.—is more appealing to you than the work project you're required to complete and which is due very soon. You may find yourself utterly willing and easily able to complete many other necessary and mundane tasks (as long as they're not the work project with its looming deadline).

So, doing nothing means being idle and failing to make any progress toward accomplishing the task to which you've been assigned or which you've set yourself.

In addition to those who do nothing in comparison to their peers and manage to get promoted anyway, there are other individuals who do nothing most of the time, so it seems like they're always doing nothing. However, these folks are the type of people who do some of their best work under pressure. That is, by procrastinating and doing nothing for most of the time (and projecting the image to others that nothing's being done), these people get quite a bit done once they start to work, causing them to be more productive in a much shorter amount of time and resulting in their promotion.

In such cases, the promotion or advancement may not be undeserved and earned on the backs of the other people. Rather, other people may not believe that the individual deserves that promotion because although they've done the necessary work to deserve it, fellow employees barely ever see that individual working. This is because they procrastinate most of the time and finish the work in a speedy and unseen manner right before the deadline, leading to the general impression that they're basically doing nothing.

So, in the context of this book, the idea of doing nothing includes not only the version of doing nothing from Chapter 3 but also the concept of doing nothing when applied in the extreme (and when used to the detriment of others) in addition to the concept of projecting the image or impression that one's doing nothing, yet being quite successful once they begin to work.

Herein lies the major problem with considering a successful implementation of the strategy in Chapter 12 to be the ultimate goal. One of the most important parts of this book is the strategy of doing nothing, and, by extension, the strategy of doing nothing and getting promoted. In fact, the concepts of doing nothing and of doing nothing and getting promoted form the foundation for a number (or, one could argue, for all) of the other strategies contained within the book, such as how to stay safe, how to claim the credit for the work of your colleagues, how to claim the credit for the work of everyone around you, and how to be a sycophant, among others. Hence, the core of this book revolves around the concept of inactivity, alongside its counterpart—the strategy of idleness leading to promotion.

But if you consider taking over the Number One job (successfully betraying the existing CEO of a company and becoming the CEO yourself, for example) as the ultimate goal and final successful implementation of all the strategies of immoral employees which I've detailed in this book, you're forgetting one crucial matter: The Number One of a company bears a lot of responsibility. A CEO has to do a lot of work. They won't be able to sustain the practice of doing nothing.

So, even if one successfully implements the strategy found in Chapter 12 of this book and is able to betray Number One and, by doing so, get the top job at the company, they won't be able to maintain their cherished practice of doing nothing (and definitely won't be able to continue practicing doing nothing and getting promoted, since there's no higher position at the company for them to be promoted to). The Number One at a company ultimately bears a lot of responsibility and must be fairly busy (busy doing *actual work*, not just *looking busy*).

The Number One at a company will inevitably face a great deal of stress and is at greater risk of suffering from burnout. All the responsibility ultimately falls on their shoulders. So in reality, being the CEO or Number One at a company isn't an ideal situation for the type of employee described in this book, one who wants to get as much as possible while offering as little as possible and get as far as possible by doing nothing. A CEO has to *do* something. And in most cases, the CEO has to do quite a lot. So being the CEO (especially for an extended period, but we'll get to that later) is antithetical to one of the defining principles of this book.

Also, the Number One at the company is almost always its most visible face (in many cases, the public face), so it's difficult or even impossible for the Number One to fly under the radar.

And let's not forget this important fact: The CEO of a company is almost always the one who's held ultimately responsible for any of its failures. Often, when a company makes a misstep or has a public failure, the CEO (or the person in the Number One position, whatever their title may be) is the one who ends up getting fired. Was it directly their fault? Almost certainly not. The fault usually lies with one of the many employees who work under them.

Consider the example of a data breach. Often, if a data breach occurs (and the public finds out about it), the CEO, the Number One at the company, or another top-ranking executive is fired or forced to resign or 'retire'. The same goes for any number of company failures, such as the failure of a product, poor sales performances for several quarters (or over the course of a year), discriminatory hiring practices, or sexual harassment lawsuits. The one who takes the blame for these failures is almost always the person who has the Number One position—yet it may not be the Number One's fault at all. They may not have known anything about the problem, mistake, or failure. But simply because they're Number One, the ultimate responsibility lies squarely on them. They thus often become the scapegoat and receive the greatest share of the blame for the failures of the company and of lesser employees, whether that blame is deserved or not.

Why is this problematic (besides the obvious drawback of potentially getting blamed and fired more easily)? Doesn't the CEO get paid enough, with enough perks to more than make up for any of these drawbacks? Well, to figure out why being the CEO is problematic, you have to recall one of the other central and foundational tenets of this text: staying safe.

Let's recall the definition of staying safe (also known as playing it safe) from Chapter 5:

In the context of this chapter, 'being safe' or 'staying safe' refers to the practice of creating a safe and stable work environment for yourself. The ideal environment is one in which you don't become embroiled in office politics or any disputes with your coworker, and in which you maintain reasonable expectations and a set of goals and achievements which are actually feasible and attainable for you and can be maintained over a long period for the sake of your career. Staying safe involves doing the tasks you are assigned in a proper manner and looking busy all the time.

As you've no doubt realized by now, maintaining and increasing your degree of safety, stability and security within your company is a vital part of this book. Safety and stability at one's workplace are key reasons why many employees prefer a system of bureaucracy (which we will cover in depth in the following chapter) to a more daring approach or system at work. And maintaining one's safety and stability at work is surely one of the primary objectives for the type of employee described in this book.

Thus, being the CEO of a company (or the person in the Number One position) is utterly problematic, because the CEO's job is essentially not very safe. In a sense, the Number One is actually one of the most vulnerable positions, because it's so visible and because the Number One usually gets blamed and is at a much greater risk of getting fired when anything goes wrong. Further, not only will the Number One get fired, but they may also face public disgrace. They may be shunned by any other company and may have trouble finding another job. They almost certainly will never be trusted to work as a CEO ever again.

So, to sum it all up, not only does being the CEO of a company usually mean needing to do a great deal of work (which is the opposite of doing nothing), but it also generally means a less safe job with much more responsibility and blame (which is the opposite of being safe). Thus, being the CEO or Number One at a company isn't usually the kind of thing that the type of employee described in this book would care to do.

What, then, was the point of Chapter 12? If immoral employees wouldn't seek to be the Number One of a company, then why is a chapter on betraying Number One and winning (with the optimal goal of becoming the replacement for the former Number One) in the book? Here is why. Being Number One isn't necessarily antithetical to the principles of doing nothing and staying safe. *Staying* Number One is where the problem actually lies. In fact, if one successfully implements all the strategies found in this book (including the one in this chapter), one could say that the ultimate goal is to become the CEO at one company ... but then to change jobs and become the CEO of *another* company before the first company discovers that you've been doing basically nothing all this time. And if the second company didn't work out, you find a job as a CEO of a *third* company, leaving the second one before you get discovered or exposed.

Some people have actually done this. And once you've been the CEO of two or three companies, there are plenty of companies who'd hire you based purely on the fact that you've been the CEO of more than one company.

Do you see how this works? The ultimate goal is to get as high as possible while doing as little work as possible and staying as safe as possible. And you should ideally do this in as short a time as possible, so that the people at your company don't have time to figure out what you're doing. Then, before they discover your strategies, you move on to the next company with a higher position and better pay and implement your strategies afresh.

This CEO job-hopping cycle is obviously not sustainable for an extended period. Being CEO for two or three different companies makes you seem like a highly successful executive, but being CEO for five to ten different companies starts to look suspicious. (Companies will be much less likely to hire you if you've already been a CEO at four different companies; they'll begin to question your commitment to the company and whether or not you'll stay with them long enough to make a meaningful impact.)

So an ideal implementation of the strategies in this book doesn't include Chapter 10, at first. If you like, you can exclude Chapter 11 as well, at first. It may be better to work your way up the ladder more slowly. And once you ascend one or two rungs, you can find a new job. At the new job, you can ascend one or two more rungs. And so on and so forth.

You can begin implementing the strategy in Chapter 11 when you're about five to fifteen years away from retirement (depending on how long you want to remain at each company). Once you successfully implement the strategy in Chapter 11 to the point of actually becoming Number Two, you can stay in the Number Two job for a few years (up to five or ten) under the radar, since the Number Two job is safer than the Number One job and usually doesn't get much of the blame. After having stayed in the Number Two job for a number of years, if you want to end your career as the CEO of a company, you can begin implementing the strategy outlined in Chapter 12 and aim for the top job. Once you get the CEO job, you can avoid doing much work and bearing too much responsibility by looking for and moving to a better opportunity (another CEO job) at another company. And once you've accepted your second CEO job, you can either retire gracefully (with plenty of money in the bank, bonuses, and perks) or try to go on to a third CEO job (after which you can finally retire in safety and peace).

This is the ultimate implementation, the dream application of all the strategies and principles contained within this book.

Don't get me wrong. It isn't easy—especially once you get to the strategies in Chapters 11 and 12 as well as the CEO job-hopping portions that combine Chapters 12 and 13). And you can't accomplish this by doing absolutely nothing. You'll have to do at least a little bit of work (whether it's by looking busy, being on the lookout for opportunities, learning arguments, learning enough about the project to take credit in a credible fashion, etc.). But it will be work that maximizes your rewards. And if you're not actively seeking a higher position but are simply looking for a good income, safety and stability, many strategies in this book will also help you to achieve that.

But enough of the grand strategy. Let's dive into the content for this chapter, which involves finding a better job before they discover that you've been doing nothing all these years.

WHY SHOULD YOU LEARN HOW TO FIND A BETTER JOB BEFORE THEY DISCOVER YOUR DECEIT?

You'll learn how to read people better.

In the process of learning how to find a better job before people discover that you've been slacking off, you'll learn new ways to read your coworkers.

Since your job is ultimately to outclass others, you must always seek new ways to stay ahead of your potential competition. Why must you learn how to read people? Well, you've hopefully realized by now that you're not the only one pursuing a similar agenda—not by a long shot. So, it's essential that you develop the ability to read people. You need to learn how to read your fellow employees, those who work under you, your boss, and even the higher-ups at your company.

If you haven't done so already, I'd highly recommend that you watch the *Lie to Me* television series. Unfortunately, it lasted just three seasons, but it's hands down one of the best shows I've ever seen. It's true to the bone.

You'll become more aware of your surroundings and highly alert as a person.

Learning how to find a better job before they discover that you've been doing nothing all these years will enable you to maintain and even heighten your sense of awareness.

As was mentioned earlier, there are always people who are seeking to outclass you and beat you at your own game, so to speak (in this instance, by seeking to take your job away from you). Thus, you must always be 'on the prowl' for opportunities, for anything that will enable you to change to a different job before you're discovered and exposed as a fraud or as someone who does basically nothing.

You'll improve your communication skills.

Attempting to find a better job before they discover that you've been doing nothing all these years will force you to improve your communication skills. Needless to say, you'll almost certainly be required to participate in interviews, so you'll need to convince the others that you are in fact a walking pile of talents and skills and that they'll suffer a great loss if they don't manage to get you.

You'll learn persistence and perseverance (even through repeated failures).

Trying to find a better job before they discover that you've been doing nothing all these years encourages you to continue to learn (even from your failures). So, it's not necessary to succeed in that first, second, or even third interview. Don't feel angry at or disappointed in yourself.

Remember: You *need* to leave your current company before you're found out, so *learn* from your mistakes. In fact, if possible, ask the ones who interviewed you for feedback on why they didn't choose you, since this gives you the opportunity to learn from your mistakes.

You'll eventually reduce the amount of work that you have to do.

In all probability, once you have the necessary experience, you'll always be able to get others to do your work for you. Step by step, you'll be able to get there. Use the experience you've gained through the implementation of the strategies in this book and make it work to your advantage.

AN ALTERNATIVE POINT OF VIEW

According to *Careers Advice Online*, those who change their jobs less than once every three years are a minority.

HOW CAN YOU FIND A BETTER JOB BEFORE THEY DISCOVER THAT YOU'VE BEEN DOING NOTHING ALL THESE YEARS? EXACTLY HOW WELL DOES THIS WORK IN THE REAL WORLD?

By making yourself look exceedingly prepared at your interview for your new job

A former employee of mine left the company, but he knew exactly where he wanted to go, so he prepared a PESTLE analysis of his target company. The people at that company were so impressed with his dedication that they offered him the job on the spot. Before they saw him for who he was, he'd changed jobs again.

PESTLE Analysis

Political **Economic** Social **Technological** **Legal** Environmental

By using the one-minute rule to be ever-prepared with concise answers

A former employee of mine used the 'one-minute rule' for any response she gave. She told me afterwards that she always practiced her responses to common interview questions and questions at presentations or staff meetings with a timer in front of the mirror. Regardless of the question asked, she always provided answers which were short and to the point. She was that good.

By fleshing out and perfecting your resume and curriculum vitae

Learn to build an awesome resume. If you always have one foot out the door of the company, you *must* have an amazing CV. Use online resources like rezscore.com see how you're doing in terms of your resume and what you can improve. Use a little of the time in which you're doing nothing at your present job to perfect and polish your resume so you can find a new job with relative ease.

Despite having been discovered by my bosses and not receiving a positive recommendation, finding a better job seems unlikely for me until they realize I've been productive all these years.

It's always good not to burn bridges, if possible. But, if this is no longer possible, you can let the other company know about the *Gallup* poll noted at the beginning of this chapter, which states that seventy-five percent of employees leave their jobs because of their bosses, not the jobs themselves. So you can explain away your lack of a good recommendation with the rationalization that your boss was a bad one.

While facing multiple rejections, the question arises about whether it's time to consider leaving my current job. The concern is that finding a better opportunity may take time, and there's a fear that my current lack of significant accomplishments could be discovered.

It's all about your priorities. Try to apply for positions based on the company rather than the position itself. A great company will always present better opportunities. And, as Wayne Gretzky said, 'You miss one hundred percent of the shots you don't take'. So it's better to try than it is to just sit at your current job, waiting to be exposed as a fraud.

Concerns may arise about the possibility of the new company uncovering my lack of productivity sooner than my current employer. Should I seek a new job before my current company becomes aware of my recent inactivity?

It's up to you to update your abilities accordingly so that this doesn't happen. Remember what I said in the beginning? You need to evolve constantly in your practices and the implementation of these strategies.

FINDING A BETTER JOB BEFORE THEY DISCOVER THAT YOU'VE BEEN DOING NOTHING ALL THESE YEARS—THE BOTTOM LINE

Most people change their jobs on a fairly frequent basis, so finding a better job before your company discovers that you've been doing nothing all these years probably won't even be noticed.

People change their jobs a lot. Those who don't are actually in the minority, not the majority. You can take advantage of this high turnover rate to net yourself a better job at a different company without anyone discovering you or questioning your motives.

You can become exceedingly skilled and practiced at finding a better job before they discover that you've been doing nothing all these years.

With practice, an employee can become superb at covering their tracks. The best 'forgers' can't be found or discovered even years after they've left the company.

A wide range of online resources can help you to find a better job before they discover that you've been doing nothing all these years.

You can utilize the vast number of free online resources, ranging from rezscore.com (for your resume) to dresscodeguide.com, to know exactly how you can prepare yourself for the time when you actually decide to leave.

CHAPTER 14
HOW 'BUREAUCRAZY' ARE YOU?

*Bureaucracy, the rule of no one, has become
the modern form of despotism.*

— MARY MCCARTHY

In this chapter, I'll be trying to assess your own level of 'bureaucrazy', whether or not you're part of a private or government organization.

SO WHAT IS BUREAUCRACY, ANYWAY? WHAT DO I MEAN WHEN I ASK, 'HOW "BUREAUCRAZY" ARE YOU?'

We come at last to the matter of bureaucracy and of being 'bureaucrazy'. But how exactly is bureaucracy defined? And what does it mean to be bureaucrazy?

In the context of this book, bureaucracy takes on the following dictionary definitions—[An] excessively complicated administrative procedure or a system of administration marked by officialism, red tape and proliferation. (Red tape, in case you need a reminder, is a figure of speech denoting official rules and processes which may delay results and which seem unnecessary.) In common parlance, bureaucracy has come to denote a highly inefficient, near-impenetrable system of laws, ordinances, regulations, and red tape that suppresses creativity and independent thought. But in this chapter, I'll detail the ways in which bureaucracy can actually be beneficial and, yes, even potentially foster creativity and independent thought.

Next, we will discuss being bureaucrazy. What on earth does this mean? One way in which the term may be defined is as follows: Bureaucrazy is any process or organization that sacrifices intelligence and rational thought in favor of administrative red tape. But this definition may be a bit too negative and limiting for the purposes of this book. So when bureaucrazy (when used as a noun) or bureaucracy is discussed in this book, let's add to it the consideration that it's a system which levels the playing field for most or all employees; that it creates a greater level of predictability, safety and job security; that it makes otherwise unfamiliar environments more easily navigable; that it allows its adherents to fit in better, no matter where they may end up; and that it generates consistent, predictable, and dependable results and best practices through repetition.

> *The purpose of bureaucracy is to compensate for incompetence and a lack of discipline.*
>
> — JAMES C COLLINS

And being bureaucrazy is to take advantage of a system of bureaucracy in order to enhance your degree of safety, stability, security, income, and comfort within your workplace. So, although the term bureaucrazy has somewhat of a negative connotation within society, being bureaucrazy is actually a good thing (at least when considered in the context of this book).

WHY DO PEOPLE TRY TO BE BUREAUCRATIC? WHAT BENEFITS DOES BUREAUCRACY CONFER ON ITS PROPONENTS AND ON THOSE WHO PRACTICE IT?

Being bureaucratic discourages the practice of playing favorites

Being bureaucratic discourages favoritism, and this impersonal nature of bureaucratic business relationships tends to favor those who are more dedicated to their job (rather than those who may be more social or better at networking). In a nutshell, everyone has the same chance to succeed when the system is bureaucratic, particularly when it comes to private corporations.

Bureaucracy usually provides a greater degree of job security for all.

A bureaucratic structure tends to provide additional job security for all those who are involved in it. Indeed, implementing and maintaining a bureaucratic structure provides a greater degree of safety and job security, because all the additional red tape ensures that very little (if anything) will fall through the cracks and potentially endanger someone's job.

Bureaucracy enables the creation of best practices through frequent and consistent repetition.

Bureaucracy can create best practices by necessitating constant repetition. Although best practices can generally take a significant amount of time to establish, ultimately, bureaucracy helps to solidify and speed up the process of establishing best practices, which will create predictable and reliable results.

Bureaucracy helps you to better fit into most types of environments.

Bureaucracy makes it easier for people to fit into a given environment and will generally end up making any kind of environment or situation more familiar. Even if someone's just started a new job in a completely different position, department or field, if both the old job and the new job have some degree of bureaucracy in place, the new employee won't feel too unfamiliar or uncomfortable in their new surroundings. This is because bureaucracy will lend an air of familiarity to the otherwise new and unfamiliar situation.

Basically, bureaucracy allows you to know where you land and where you stand.

Bureaucracy generates a greater degree of predictability.

Bureaucracy creates predictability. Simply put, it makes outcomes more predictable merely because the results are more reliable and consistent as opposed to the ones you'd get in a scenario in which bureaucracy isn't in place.

AN ALTERNATIVE POINT OF VIEW

Bureaucracy is the death of every achievement.

—ALBERT EINSTEIN

HOW DO PEOPLE BECOME BUREAUCRAZY OR PRACTICE BUREAUCRACY? WHAT ARE SOME OF THE ILLUSTRATIONS OF BEING BUREAUCRATIC, BEING A PART OF A BUREAUCRACY, OR FOSTERING A SYSTEM OF BUREAUCRACY?

Remaining part of a bureaucratic system can engender greater job safety and security.

Many of my former employees actually decided to turn down the opportunity to lead working teams when they were given it, stating that they prefer instead to be a cog in the system, just one of the many parts working together to create a well-oiled machine. Few of them prefer to assume responsibility. Instead, they'll rather have someone else take the blame if things go south and allow the responsibility to fall on them. They prefer bureaucracy, a familiar, safe and predictable environment.

Staying a part of a system of bureaucracy reduces your level of risk and offers greater income stability.

It may seem strange that I'm able to use so many of my former employees as examples in this chapter, but it just goes to show how comfortable, safe, and secure it can be to remain in a system of bureaucracy.

Many of my former employees have said that they'd actually prefer a smaller yet stable income as opposed to, say, being given shares of the company. Their responses, almost always, are invariably the same: They have a mortgage, they have to send their kids to school or college, they have a relative who's ill, and so on and so forth. These and other similar reasons are almost always their rationale for preferring a stable income over something more lucrative but potentially riskier.

Stability, not the potentially enormous amount of money they could make (tied to a proportionally enormous level of risk and responsibility), is what matters to these types of employees the most. And there's no shame in being such an employee. I certainly appreciated their efforts. There would be no well-oiled machine without cogs such as these.

Taking advantage of the benefits offered by a bureaucratic system will keep you protected.

The majority of people I know have come to appreciate the system of bureaucracy for its benefits. I even have an acquaintance who says the following: 'Always make sure you're covered with papers. Not even a bullet can cross through a signed paper'. Although the phrasing may be a bit blunt, I can see the logic behind it and the reason why so many people appreciate bureaucracy for its benefits, which aren't so few in number. This red tape, those signed sheets of paper, provide a high degree of security and stability to all those involved.

SOME OBJECTIONS TO BEING 'BUREAUCRAZY' AND RESPONSES TO THOSE OBJECTIONS

The existing bureaucratic system tends to discourage individuals from acquiring new skills.

It may be true that bureaucracy doesn't encourage individuals to gain new skills. But then again, there's very little that actually does encourage people to do so. Thus, if you rely on bureaucracy for anything other than safety, you'll find yourself at a loss. Don't put too much stock in the system of bureaucracy. It's just what it is, nothing more and nothing less.

In an environment characterized by bureaucracy, procrastination tends to be fostered.

Again, this is actually up to the individual. If an individual seeks to progress as a human being and learn new things instead of procrastinating, they'll do so regardless of their position. And if an individual wants to procrastinate, they'll definitely also do so, regardless of whether there's a system of bureaucracy in place or not.

Speaking of work environments, it's worth noting that bureaucracy tends to limit an individual's freedom.

As was mentioned earlier, some employees are just fine with not having such a great degree of freedom. In fact, if these individuals are given too much freedom, they won't know what to do with it or how to act. Believe me—I've tried to give them more freedom, but have almost always been disappointed with the results. These employees are fine with being part of the decision. They certainly don't mind being involved, as long as the ultimate responsibility doesn't lie with them.

HOW 'BUREAUCRAZY' ARE YOU?— THE BOTTOM LINE

Being a bureaucrat or part of a bureaucracy isn't actually as bad as it may sound.

There are instances in which the system of bureaucracy does quite well, so being a bureaucrat isn't all that bad. Bureaucracy creates a predictable environment and a more familiar one at that. Thus, it will end up creating a more knowledgeable and comfortable working environment.

Many employees who reach a certain level will crave bureaucracy and the stability it brings.

Once employees reach a certain level of experience, stability frequently becomes much more important than the amount of money they make, for various reasons.

Being a part of a bureaucracy can sometimes engender creativity.

As strange as it may seem, bureaucracy can encourage creativity, particularly for those who are genuinely willing to help others. If all employees in a bureaucracy feel safe and stable due to the system of which they're a part, some may feel freer to help others and hold brainstorming sessions to help the company run more smoothly.

If these employees are made to feel safe and secure (and not worried about their job security), they may be more willing to help each other instead of being wary of one another and seeking to climb up above one another.

CONCLUSION

In the journey through this guidebook, we've explored the art of doing nothing and witnessed its evolution into strategic maneuvers for success. From the early stages of mastering the subtle skill of idleness to the complex tactics of betraying superiors and claiming undeserved credit, we've uncovered a spectrum of workplace behaviors. As we reflect on the various strategies outlined in each chapter—from becoming an adept sycophant to skillfully navigating the intricate web of office politics—it becomes evident that success, in this unconventional sense, requires a combination of wit, cunning, and an understanding of the intricacies of 'bureaucrazy'.

Ultimately, this guidebook isn't a prescription for ethical or commendable conduct; instead, it serves as a satirical exploration of the extreme possibilities within a bureaucratic environment. As we conclude our journey through these chapters, readers may find a sense of closure, realizing the exaggerated nature of the scenarios presented. The underlying message remains clear: Success should ideally be achieved through dedication, integrity, and genuine contributions. The humorous exploration of office dynamics, as outlined in these chapters, encourages reflection on the importance of ethical behavior in the pursuit of professional success.

AUTHOR BIO

SULTAN ALSHAALI PROFILE

Sultan accumulated extensive knowledge and experience in various areas, including strategic planning, organizational development, manufacturing, education, entrepreneurship, coaching and mentoring, being a Clifton Strength Team coach, and a Co-active coach focusing on continuous self-development and improvement of others, as well as being a published author and public speaker.

Sultan holds two master's degrees, an MBA in Business Administration in Entrepreneurship from Liverpool University in the UK and a professional master's degree in business Strategy and Development from City & Guilds in the UK and many other honors and awards. He is also a graduate of the UAE Government Leadership Program, Executive Leadership of the 21st Century, a model based on three pillars: Leadership spirit, outlook and Achievements and impact.

Sultan Alshaali is the Chairman and CEO of Alabjadeya Investment, an agile and diversified investment firm with an extensive portfolio of young innovative businesses worldwide. With a focus on start-ups and maximizing opportunities by developing companies from a setup with inventive entrepreneurs.

He is also the Vice President of Business Development at the International Accelerator, looking after the Middle East and North Africa region. Identifying, incubating, and rapidly developing unique, innovative startups projects, initiatives, and services with a potential exponential social impact, sustainability, and scalability.

He was the Founding Director of the Government Accelerators in the UAE Prime Minister's Office, establishing and overseeing the operations of the world's first Government Accelerators a platform for cross-sectoral teams that focuses on challenges and delivers tangible results in short periods, eliminating the silo work mindset and empowering multi-stakeholders' collaboration.

Since 2011, Sultan has been volunteering on the Board of Directors of the World Congress of Muslim Philanthropists, a global network of affluent individuals, foundations, and socially responsible corporations established to advance effective and accountable giving.

Sultan is also volunteering on the Board of Directors of Al Noor Rehabilitation & Welfare Association for People of Determination, a non-profit organization providing outstanding learning experiences to enrich the lives of children and young adults with various physical and cognitive.

He was also an Executive Board Member of Ajman Modern School, the first international school of the Northern Emirates, an associate member of the UNESCO and Counsels of International Schools as well as an Executive Board Member of the AS group, a third-generation family enterprise that pioneered fiberglass boat and yachts design and manufacturing in the Middle East and expanded to different industries.

Notes

www.ingramcontent.com/pod-product-compliance
Lightning Source LLC
Chambersburg PA
CBHW030104240426
43661CB00001B/12